THE BLISS OF STRUGGLE

THE BLISS OF STRUGGLE

WINNING STRATEGIES
FOR DEMANDING TIMES

BY

KURT GASSNER

My-mindguide.com

The Bliss of Struggle
Kurt Gassner

Impressum
My-mindguide – The publishing trademarke of trendguide Capital GmbH, Klenzestr. 42a, 80469 Munich, Germany.

Reg. Nr. HRB Munich 206639, VAT 152 123 159, CEO: Kurt Friedrich Gassner
Web: www.my-mindguide.com, mail: gassner@my-mindguide.com

Paperback ISBN: 978-3-98793-914-3
Hardback ISBN: 978-3-949978-71-5

Table of Contents

Struggles

My-mindguide.com

Introduction

"When you walk to the edge of all the light you have and take that first step into the darkness of the unknown, you must believe that one of two things will happen. There will be something solid for you to stand upon or you will be taught to fly."

~ *Patrick Overton*, The Leaning Tree: [poems]

A seed is planted in the ground and watered. Almost immediately, it begins to awaken from its slumber and react to its new environment. Though it appears completely dead and lifeless outside of the soil, it comes alive and does the most unbelievable things once it has been planted. It cannot be seen by those above ground without special camera technology. But beneath the surface, an almost magical process is taking place — one that we take for granted because it is happening simultaneously around the world billions of times.

We see the growth of plants as routine and mundane when it is quite extraordinary. That seed uses the benefit of deep, dark soil to construct the building blocks for the rest of its life cycle. It turns out that plants require darkness as much as they require light. Darkness signals them to perform certain functions that are essential for their lives over the long term.

By the fourth week of pregnancy, babies have not perceived any light as their tiny visual systems are formed. It will take a few more weeks before light, mostly red hues, can penetrate the mother's belly. Then, four weeks later, eyelids are formed to cover the baby's new eyes and plunge it back into a place where light must struggle to reach. The next several weeks of development must be completed in darkness. For the remaining months of the pregnancy, the baby will get small infusions of light. But the darkness is critical to the development of every system in its tiny body. Less than one percent of ambient light outside the mother's belly can penetrate. It is not until the fifth or sixth month that the eyelids can separate relatively easily and signal to the baby that there is something beyond the warm waters of the womb.

The advent of digital photography has caused many to forget that old school photographers had to build dark rooms to make beautiful pictures. These rooms with hardly any light provided the perfect environment for light-sensitive materials to develop slowly and accurately.

There are a million places in our world where darkness plays an essential role. Even the earth itself is arranged so that morning follows night. Without those long-night seasons where the sun hides away and allows the moon to be the star of the show, we would not have the smooth transitions of the tides. There are places in our universe that are perpetually bright – like the sun. But there are dark places in our universe where only the faintest amount of light reaches. That darkness is a major part of the delicate balance that keeps the galaxy in place.

The contrast between light and dark is both a physical and metaphysical expression for human beings. From a natural perspective, human beings would suffer from the interruption to the flow of serotonin that comes when it is dark. Nighttime also cools the earth's temperature so that the sun does not cook the entire planet.

Beyond physical darkness, however, are the places and times in our lives when a different type of darkness touches us through sickness, fear, poverty, or death. When these dark elements reach us, we often recoil and ask why. We complain, cry, and decry the darkness. Could it be, however, that we fail to see the beauty that is available to us by way of the darkness?

So many of us fear the dark. Literal fear of the dark, or nyctophobia, afflicts millions. In the U.S. alone, 11 million people have some sort of extreme reaction to darkness, making it a more common affliction than fear of heights. But there is another fear of the dark that plagues humans that is not perceived with the human eye. It is the fear of the dark places we might find ourselves when we want to be someplace else.

In the coming pages, I will cover the dark places of poverty, sickness, loss, and fear in ways that you may have never considered before. I hope to unlock the truth that there can be extreme beauty even in dark places and that truth challenges you and makes you stronger. And what makes you stronger makes you unstoppable.

To be born on the dark side can make you tough beyond your wildest dreams. You can turn the tables on nearly any situation. In today's world, with all its changes and challenges, you can make yourself more able to survive, adapt, and be resilient.

With the right mindset, just about every cloud can reveal its silver lining. An enlightened mind can view any adversity as an opportunity. Mindset can move you from fear and overwhelm to determination and contentment. The right mindset has been proven even to impact the body. People who have been given a short time to live, for example, develop a powerful mindset toward life and are still alive a decade later. Where some are crushed by adversity, others thrive. Why? It isn't just because they are go-getters with a never-say-die attitude. It is because they learn something from their tough times that others miss.

When you have had a rough start in life, you may feel that you are being pulled in two opposing directions. One side of the universe seems to be taunting you with statistics and stories about how people who experienced a similar start ended up. And it's never good news. The other side of the universe consists of all the feel-good messages that tell you that you can abandon your past, overcome it, and become a new person. They encourage you to "change your life."

Of course, I understand what they mean, but what is the truth? You can't change your life — not the history part of it; it cannot be rewritten. And you can't change the present since you are living through it. You can only shape and guide the future. Trying to plan a future without acknowledging the past means living a sort of schizophrenic existence. You are who you are *with* your difficult past. Your past does not define you. But you are connected to it because it has led you, step-by-step, to the person you are.

Messages about following your dreams are ineffective when you are haunted by nightmares of yesterday. If you feel embarrassed, ashamed, guilt-ridden, or thwarted by your past, you will find moving forward tricky — if not impossible.

In the coming pages, I hope to show you how to engage the imagination, receive new information, change your perspective, and receive the strength to stand on the rubble of the past with an eye toward your ever-emerging future. You will feel empowered to integrate your past failures, difficulties, and yes, even embarrassment into a future that is rich and well-rounded. Through these techniques, you will learn to imagine the future by bringing your past to the present in a healthy way.

Struggles

My-mindguide.com

Chapter One

How it All Began

"Someone I loved once gave me a box full of darkness. It took me years to understand that this, too, was a gift."
~ Mary Oliver

I'm a terminal "start-up" person. Not a day goes by that I don't have a rush of ideas looking for real estate in my brain. I generally find a home for all of my ideas. Some get to move from community lodging to prime locations in the penthouse of my mind. For some, living life with this flurry of activity might generate a call to their therapist for the next available appointment. For me, it is the only way to live. The high-speed traffic taking place in my head is not only a source of exhilaration that keeps me fresh regardless of the date on my birth certificate. It also serves as a continual testament to the power of the human mind to lift us from one place to another. No matter how deep in the mud we might be at one point in our lives, if we can harness the superpowers within, our potential is limitless… and frighteningly so!

I was born into poverty. Not the kind of poverty where you still manage to have name-brand clothes and the latest smartphone. Rather, the old-fashioned type of poverty where meals were a luxury. My prospects appeared rather slim to anyone looking at me from the outside. Thankfully, my perspective was from the inside out. From there, the world was a menu, and I was sitting at its table, ready to place my order and dine on the feast it would set before me. I had no idea how I would get out of the pit of poverty, but I was convinced that, somehow, I would.

An outsider's perspective might have done an inventory of my life and found me lacking in all of the creature comforts that define wealth. But I assessed that I had talent, creativity, goals, and desire. I was sitting on an invisible king's ransom. I wasn't going to waste time with worry. I was going to get busy doing.

Besides, they don't know how I started.

I often say that being born on the dark side can make you stronger. I say this from firsthand experience. I was born shortly after the end of World War II. The world was still torn in two, and the ravages of war were evident in the cities where the war was waged. But the war had not just changed the landscape of the countries involved. It had shaped the mindset of the people who lived through it. Being raised in the 50s by parents who had seen war meant that my training as a child was different from kids whose parents had not seen war. There was a seriousness to their parenting. We made up for what we may have lacked in financial resources in determination and drive.

If I had any doubt that the war was a terribly dark period in my parents' lives, there was always the visual reminder of my father's missing leg. Both of my parents had been students. But then, my father was drafted and served in the military. He came out of the war with just one leg. There were no spoils for the soldiers of war to divide. We had absolutely no money and lived together in a one-room apartment. Work was scarce at the time, particularly for a man with a significant disability. They struggled to feed and clothe themselves. Then I was conceived.

After the war, I was born into abject poverty in Linz/Danube, Austria. Everything was in rubble. The city was split between the Russians and the U.S. Our tiny little room had no running water, no bathroom, and no toilet.

Despite their love for their new baby boy, my parents reached the point where they could not afford to keep me. They just couldn't manage it unless they both worked, leaving no one to care for me. So, with broken hearts, they gave me to an orphanage, or a baby sanctuary, when I was just twelve months old. This is where rooms full of babies live where they might at least be fed wholesome food and dressed in warm, clean clothes.

I can only imagine what it must have been like for them to walk away from their baby, not knowing if I would be held and loved or if they would ever see me again. It was a terribly dark time for them and a dark era for the whole world. So many babies had to be abandoned and given away.

I remained in the baby sanctuary until I reached the age of three. Even at that early age, I was aware of the struggles that separated me from my family. We were finally reunited, but the poverty we labored under continued. There was a series of ups and downs that were so devastating that it eventually strained my parents' marriage.

The next years were a terrible struggle. My father was a young breadwinner for three children and a wife who moved from one job to another trying to provide for us. Life was stressful and, when I was just eight, they split up for one year. We moved to Austria. After one year, my parents decided to attempt to piece their marriage back together. We moved to Germany, but the change of scenery was not enough to heal the divide between them. It was obvious that divorce was close.

When I was thirteen, we moved to a sad little house in Traun, Austria. It was always cold and extremely uncomfortable. I spent a lot of time alone because my mother had to work, leaving me with the grown-up responsibility of caring for three siblings.

I attended school, but it was clear that I was not living a similar life to my classmates. Life is not easy when you are the only one in the class who can't afford to go on the school excursions. My life changed when my parents enrolled me in a beautiful boarding school. I breathed a sigh of relief to be in such comfortable surroundings and looked forward to staying there for the rest of my education. Unfortunately, just one year later, my hopes were dashed. My father couldn't afford the monthly payments, and I was forced to leave.

At the age of sixteen, I was old enough to work, so it was time for me to leave home and go out into the world independently.

My birth happened during a tragic time, I spent my younger years away from the people who loved me, and now I was just a teenager having to fend for myself in the world alone. It was hard, but I knew I would make it. I was more resilient because I had already lived many years in the basement of society.

I found a furnished room in a boarding house where I lived alone. At the age of seventeen, I enlisted in the military primarily because they offered a salary, food, and lodging. At the age of eighteen, I started my quest to climb the social ladder with the goal of reaching the very top.

When I say I wasn't born with a golden spoon, I say it with authority. I can also say with authority that it is the responsibility of every person to make the best of the problems handed to them by life. I decided that I had spent enough years on the dark side of life. I had paid whatever dues life decided I must pay. It was time to reinvent myself. That is precisely what I did.

The path of reinvention was long and hard. But I was strong enough to meet the task head-on because I had been born into times that were equally long and hard. I was no stranger to the dark side. The difference was that I was a helpless child the first time. This time, even though I would be driving in the dark, I had my hand firmly on the steering wheel. I was in control.

I was able to do whatever I wanted. I desired a beautiful life with a lovely home. I wanted to be financially secure. I accomplished that. From each achievement, I set a new goal.

I want to stress that people who have started life on the dark side, or been plunged into darkness, can still have their dreams come true. There is no shame in poverty. Poverty teaches you gratitude for everything you receive. Poverty keeps you alert to every opportunity. Poverty builds character. And poverty keeps you hungry for more, not physically but figuratively. I always wanted more because I knew that I had what it took to achieve a better life.

You can create the life you want. I see a lot of my contemporaries have reached their 60s and 70s. They complain about being bored. Many of them have started drinking to combat the boredom and silence the voices of their dreams calling out to them to get busy living. They lament that they spent their 20s, 30s, 40s, and 50s working and building careers. Once they retired, they didn't know what to do with themselves. The rest of their lives are purposeless and empty. They are stuck.

I want to encourage the young readers to get in hot pursuit of their dreams now while they are young. I want to encourage older readers by letting them know that their lives are not over. As long as you have breath, you have opportunity. Even if your health is declining and your mind is a bit fuzzy, you can reinvent yourself. You may be surprised to find that when you get busy living, your brain waves start to fire again. Your increased activity may help your body regain its strength. Most importantly, you can satisfy the longings of your heart by doing what you crave.

Chapter Two

The Gift of Poverty

"That same night, I wrote my first short story. It took me thirty minutes. It was a dark little tale about a man who found a magic cup and learned that if he wept into the cup, his tears turned into pearls. But even though he had always been poor, he was a happy man and rarely shed a tear. So, he found ways to make himself sad so that his tears could make him rich. As the pearls piled up, so did his greed grow. The story ended with the man sitting on a mountain of pearls, knife in hand, weeping helplessly into the cup with his beloved wife's slain body in his arms."

~ Khaled Hosseini, The Kite Runner

Poverty is one of the dark places people often cite as inciting terror in their hearts. Perhaps they were born poor and were reared in a place of struggle and financial challenges. Or maybe they had poverty thrust upon them at the loss of a job, an accident, an illness, or a death. However poverty comes, there is no argument over the fact that it is not easy to navigate. People who experience it must learn to adapt to a world that seems to thrive on money. How do you survive or succeed when money is the standard of success, and you have none?

Modern society, especially in the western world, is structured so that poverty is considered a fate worse than death. In a world that runs on economies, money is the essential component. However, there is a price to pay (pardon the pun) for a world where money is the driving force. One of the downsides is that people born into poverty assume that they are significantly worse off than those born into money.

People born poor are socialized to believe one of two narratives. They can settle into the statistics about poverty in their part of the world, relegating themselves to a state of "doing the best I can." Or they can adopt a motivated attitude that spurs them to try to escape their poverty. Whichever way they choose to direct their lives, society will judge them by their choice. In most countries, the poor are juxtaposed against the rich. And it is only in such an environment that poverty can be measured. If we all have a hut, none of us can claim to be better off than the other. In fact, I might love my hut until you build a brick house next door.

One Virginia community wanted to test this theory to determine if poverty is indeed relative and prove that humans can learn to live among each other without wealth playing a role. This community of Twin Oaks, Virginia seems to have caught lightning in a bottle. But it is not sheer luck that accounts for its success. They intentionally created a society where money plays little to no role. In their blog, they write:

…We divide our work equally and share our income from the businesses we collectively own. Income sharing means that we pool together all the money we make and meet the needs of the group from this income. All the work of the members is evaluated the same, an hour is an hour.

Most members do not touch or deal with money at all most days. Your commitment to the community is 42 hours per week - if you do that, the community covers all your living costs such as food, housing, medical, education, entertainment, transportation, etc.

We do get a small $100 per month allowance with which we buy the things that the community does not purchase for us (perhaps cigarettes or chocolate or alcohol, though the community does buy some of the latter two).

It is like living in a little self-sustaining village, where everyone knows each other. Most members do not leave the community on most days, and for most, this is not a hardship. There is no live television and no advertising except what one sees on the internet and in magazines.

We do not have property crime, real poverty, or homelessness (unlike the rest of the U.S., where these are significant problems). It is a slower pace of life than many places. We eat organic food that we grow ourselves, raise our own kids, take care of our own elders, build our own buildings, fix our own cars, and run our own businesses.

***

More money does not mean more happiness, as many poor people assume. This false belief causes them to think that they will become wealthy and happy if they could just win the lottery, create a popular invention, start a winning business, or write a book or song that sweeps the nation. Studies show, however, that even if you are richer, you are not necessarily happier.

Researchers were seeking to explain why people in rich nations have not become any happier on average over the last forty years, even though economic growth has led to substantial increases in average incomes.

Lead researcher on the paper, Chris Boyce, from the University of Warwick's Department of Psychology, said: "Our study found that the ranked position of an individual's income best predicted general life satisfaction, while the actual amount of income and the average income of others appear to have no significant effect." The study entitled "Money and Happiness: Rank of Income, Not Income, Affects Life Satisfaction" will be published in the journal Psychological Science. The researchers looked at data on earnings and life satisfaction from seven years of the British Household Panel Survey (BHPS), which is a representative longitudinal sample of British households.

First, they examined how life satisfaction was related to how much money each person earned. They found, however, that satisfaction was much more strongly related to the ranked position of the person's income (compared to people of the same gender, age, level of education, or from the same geographical area).

The results explain why making everybody in society richer will not necessarily increase overall happiness – because it is only having a higher income than other people that matters.

~Chris Boyce, Gordon Brown (both of the University of Warwick's Department of Psychology), and Simon Moore of Cardiff University

***

If you have ever had a conversation with someone who was desperately poor, you would learn that, although they do not enjoy the creature comforts we have grown to view as essential, they have a rich perspective of the world that can't be experienced when chasing the next dollar or the latest version of the iPhone.

One homeless person in Britain posted the following:

The more I ponder upon it, the more I become cognizant of the fact that poverty is not "another world." It's another dimension.

We live in the grey, the sepia-toned. Thousands of tiny decisions are made for us by indigence and our survival within it.

When I was young, solvent, and employed, I would watch planes fly and imagine all the wonderful places in the world that I would visit one day. Kathmandu, Timbuktu, Paris, Egypt – the list went on.

I realized today as I walked Mojo that I hadn't looked up in years, and I consciously took a moment to watch the sky. It felt unnatural.

When you are impecunious, you are given a gift. A gift of seeing people as they really are. People are kind. People do care. It happens in a myriad of ways, unexpectedly and without fanfare. When it does, it fills your heart and overflows into your soul, and life is wonderful because you are seen. Somebody kind cares and acts accordingly.

***

My-mindguide.com

Chapter Three

A True Legacy

*"Everyone must leave something behind when he dies, my grandfather
said. A child or a book or a painting or a house or a wall built or
a pair of shoes made. Or a garden planted. Something your hand
touched some way so your soul has somewhere to go when you die,
and when people look at that tree or that flower you planted, you're
there.*

*It doesn't matter what you do, he said, so long as you change
something from the way it was before you touched it into something
that's like you after you take your hands away. The difference between
the man who just cuts lawns and a real gardener is in the touching,
he said. The lawn-cutter might just as well not have been there at all;
the gardener will be there a lifetime."*

~ Ray Bradbury, Fahrenheit 451

What do the following people have in common?
— *Warren Buffet*
— *Bill Gates*
— *Gloria Vanderbilt*
— *Sting*
— *George Lucas*
— *Mark Zuckerberg*
— *Elton John*

— *Andrew Lloyd Webber*
— *Simon Cowell*
— *Jackie Chan*

Of course, they are all famously and fabulously wealthy. Three of them are among the ten richest people in the world. But they share a more important distinction. None of them are leaving all of their fortunes to their children. The average person thinks about dying and leaving behind, at the very least, a handsome insurance policy for their children to live on and enjoy. Others work diligently to pay off their homes and other debt so that their estate is robust enough to help their children get a strong start in life. Some even admit that they do not want their children to struggle to get ahead like they had to do

They do not realize that, inherent in their desire to do well by their children, they may actually be harming them. Leaving large sums of money to children might be one of the worst things a parent can do. Living large on a parent's income can be crippling enough to a child's sense of self-dependence and drive. But when the parents pass away and leave the child large sums of money, it can be the nail in their motivational coffin.

Lynn Chen-Zhang recounts with horror the day his son came home and announced that he had no desire to study or work to get good grades. He said his classmate had noted that Chen-Zhang was a wealthy business owner, so surely his son would be taken care of for the rest of his life. Why should he bother to worry about graduating at the top of his class, going to an Ivy League college, and getting a high-paying job? His inheritance would surely eclipse any money even an executive position could pay him.

Chen-Zhang decided to change his plan to will his entire estate to his two boys. He let them know that he would care for them for the rest of their childhood and finance the best education money could buy. After that, his boys were on their own. Suddenly, they got serious about their education. Fast forward ten years, both graduated college and are working in the finance industry earning their own money.

Many people who are quite wealthy agree with the Chen-Zhang's on their stance about leaving inheritances to their children. Warren Buffet has a net worth that eclipses $100 billion. But on the topic of leaving his billions to his children, he is non-negotiable.

I'm not an enthusiast for dynastic wealth, particularly when six billion others have much poorer hands than we do in life. They've known all along my views on inherited wealth, and share them. They have money that most people dream of."

~ Warren Buffet

***

He has decided to leave 85 percent of his estate to charity. Only 15 percent will be left to his children. Yes, 15 percent split between three children is still a tidy sum.

Bill Gates was heavily influenced by Buffet's decision and is leaving his children even less. They will have to make do with less than 1 percent of their famous father's wealth. Each will receive $10 million.

"I definitely think leaving kids massive amounts of money is not a favor to them. Warren Buffett was part of an article in Fortune talking about this in 1986 before I met him, and it made me think about it and decide he was right."

***

Star Wars creator George Lucas is also in the low inheritance club. He is worth $6.5 billion. He participated in the Giving Pledge campaign, where wealthy people commit to leaving the bulk of their estates to charity. Facebook CEO Zuckerberg is cutting his kids' inheritance even shorter, promising to donate 99 percent of his wealth, leaving his kids that remaining one percent, or a billion dollars, to share.

Rock star, Sting, commented on his decision to cut his children's inheritance. Though he is worth $300 million, it will not all go to his kids. He told the Daily Mail:

"I told them there won't be much money left because we are spending it! We have a lot of commitments. What comes in we spend, and there isn't much left. I certainly don't want to leave them trust funds that are albatrosses round their necks. They have to work."

***

Martial arts expert and film star, Jackie Chan, explains why it is essential to make children work for their own money rather than live off their parents' largesse. He is giving 50 percent of his $350 million estate to charity and plans to spend the rest in his lifetime, leaving his children nothing as an inheritance:

"If [they are] capable, [they] can make [their] own money. If [they are] not, then [they] will just be wasting my money."

***

Celebrity judge, Simon Cowell, is committed to doing nothing to handicap his kids' ability to make money for themselves. He revealed plans for his half a billion-dollar fortune in an interview with The Mirror:

"I'm going to leave my money to somebody. A charity, probably – kids and dogs. I don't believe in passing [wealth] from one generation to another."

***

Superstar British singer and songwriter has a net worth that is also approaching half a billion dollars. While he is committed to taking care of his two sons, they will not be spending the bulk of it. He also shared his thoughts with The Mirror:

"Of course, I want to leave my boys in a very sound financial state. But it's terrible to give kids a silver spoon. It ruins their life. Listen, the boys live the most incredible lives; they're not normal kids, and I'm not pretending they are. But you have to have some semblance of normality, some respect for money, some respect for work."

***

Anderson Cooper of CNN fame admitted that his famous mother, Gloria Vanderbilt, did not leave him any money. He had to earn his own, which he did well with his $12 million per year CNN contract. Similarly, Phantom of the Opera composer, Andrew Lloyd Webber, will leave just a sliver of his more than one-billion-dollar net worth to his five children.

Why are these super rich people encouraging this practice of not leaving large sums of money to their children? It seems clear that they developed and have come to value the work ethic they learned from the struggle. There is great bliss in working one's way through a problem and successfully coming out on the other side. When that problem is poverty, working through it has powerful implications for the future. A person who pulls their way up from poverty has the assurance that, if they lost it all, they might be able to do it again. It creates a certain sense of security that lasts a lifetime. But there is more.

We live in a society where self-respect is a rare commodity. Fame can come from accomplishments that are less than stellar. One YouTube content creator has gotten quite wealthy by recording videos of himself sleeping. One might suspect that no one would be interested in watching a stranger sleep. However, this channel has 65,000 subscribers, and his ten-hour sleeping video has ten million views. Yet another channel shows a woman eating cereal. That's it. Just eating cereal. It has nearly 2 million views and 9 million subscribers. This may make you chuckle or cause you to fear that we are in a crisis of self-esteem and self-respect.

When a person can set up a video camera and earn $5,000 for recording himself sleeping, one wonders what that person's future will look like. Easy money brings with it the expectation that the next wave of money will be just as easy. It can set up a reckless attitude around spending and saving that is hard to overcome.

Take lottery winners, for example. What could be more thrilling than purchasing a chance lottery at the right time and the right place with the right set of numbers or scratch-off spaces that win you large sums of money for the investment of a few dollars? But, according to the National Endowment for Financial Education, seventy percent of lottery winners have lost every penny in just a few years. Thirty-three percent of that group do even worse: they lose their winnings and all the other money they had, causing them to declare bankruptcy.

This phenomenon lends credence to the claim of wealthy people that a sudden windfall would not solve all of a poor person's problems. There is some value in the struggle to become wealthy. Some are lucky to lose only their money. Many lose their lives as criminals, and (more likely) acquaintances and family members, murder them to take their newfound fortune. The lottery winners had neither the knowledge nor the time to learn the intricacies of wealth, such as how to protect themselves physically and financially. As a woover.com quote says, "The ones who don't win the lottery are the lucky ones. They are given the gift to struggle."

There is much more to being wealthy than additional zeroes in your bank balance. There are issues in connection with taxes, security, community property (if married), investments, trusts, inheritances, etc. The list goes on and on.

Our personalities are made up of our thoughts, choices, actions, beliefs, and emotional state. For example, someone who thinks the world is unfair or hostile and that everyone is selfish and dangerous will make the choices that reflect that belief. They will put themselves in positions and environments that reflect the world they expect to see.

One woman wrote anonymously that every time she went to the theatre, the person behind her kicked the back of her chair. She recounted that it happened every time without fail. She later realized that her belief system attracted the negative, repeat occurrence.

We get the world we expect to get. But this is good news when you realize that a shift in your belief system can attract a more positive outcome. Remember that the universe seeks to affirm what you believe.

Conversely, someone whose state of mind is compassionate, grateful, and creative will make choices to have experiences that are life-loving, expansive, and affirming. They will find that they are experiencing the emotions and experiences congruent with their positive thought processes. Their lives conform to the good they believe is in the world.

I can tell you that the world is a wondrous, beautiful, and magical place. I have been all over the world and seen some of the most incredible sights around the globe. Despite the issues we face politically, economically, and socially, it doesn't detract from the truth that the world is amazing and filled with friendly and loving people.

Some people who are living in the past seek to recreate in their present what they have come to expect as a result of that troubled past. But living in the present and dreaming about the future can help create a brand-new life for you. Your personality change is at the core of creating this new you. You must simply find clarity about who you want to be and how you want to live. Then you can share your life with others with the joy of knowing that you are adding value to every life you touch. This is the most incredible legacy we can give, spread, and leave behind when our time is up in the physical world.

Do you want a close and loving relationship with your spouse? Do you desire a better connection with your children or your friends? Do you want to have more exciting experiences? Do you want to travel more? Do you want to support a charity that is making a difference in the world? Your life will fall into alignment with your belief system. The universe will give you more of what you expect.

Your legacy grows to be more than just money, houses, stocks, or personal possessions. That is all good to leave behind. But your true legacy is the legacy of thought, the legacy of love, and the legacy of personal power. This comes from your construction of the brand-new version of you.

This is not a chore. It can be a labor of love — self-love. And it can be fun. Treat yourself to a black notebook and cup of coffee. Sit alone in a coffee house and create the avatar of yourself. It can be as simple as a stick figure. Or you can use an app or a site like avatarmaker.com. Then ask yourself:

- What choices would this person make?
- What actions will this person be taking?
- What beliefs does this person have about the world they live in?
- How does it feel to be her or him?
- Where does this person work?
- What do they like to do for fun?
- Who do they love romantically?

You can ask any question you want. The most important question, though, is, "How does this person impact the world?" That is your legacy.

Now it is time to embody the new you. Anytime you catch yourself in old ways of thinking, old patterns of feeling, stop and go back to your avatar. That is why it is essential to have a visual representation. If you can see it, you can be it. Perfecting the new you will require repetition over time. You are what you do repeatedly. So, keep at it until it becomes second nature.

The longer we spend connected to this new expression of self, the more we recognize the beauty of our lives and the many gifts we have to offer, even with the ups and downs, heartache, and pains. They cannot overshadow the gift that is you.

I have stayed the course and created the life of my dreams through a sense of responsibility because I was given a second chance. I should have been lost with no direction and fearful of loving and connecting with others. But I was able to dig deep and find the courage to create this version of my life. Some of the children of that orphanage went on to experience disastrous lives. It was only by developing a strong mind that I could escape that same fate.

I aligned myself with the future version that I dreamed I could be. Then, through a lot of hard work, I stepped into that future self. I know that you are strong enough, beautiful enough, and creative enough to create all you've ever dreamed of and more.

Love yourself. Trust yourself. And give yourself to the world so that you can change it for the better, one tiny gesture at a time. As more people free themselves of the self-imprisonment of their dark pasts and find the beauty present in the darkness, we can build a global community based on cooperation, understanding, compassion, expression, and equality.

What better world would there be for us to leave for the next generation, and what an incredible feeling knowing that you played your part in the evolution of human consciousness and the expansion of humanity?

Struggles

My-mindguide.com

Chapter Four

The Bliss of the Struggle

"The harder the conflict, the more glorious the triumph. What we obtain too cheap, we esteem too lightly; it is dearness only that gives everything its value. I love the man that can smile in trouble, that can gather strength from distress and grow."

~ Thomas Paine

A U.S. preschool teacher thought it would be a great idea to buy a butterfly exhibit for her four- and five-year-old students. She excitedly ordered the kit and watched impatiently for the live caterpillars and butterfly enclosure to arrive by mail. The day finally came. After a brief lesson on life cycles, she and her students erected the enclosure and released the caterpillars from their tiny box. Safely inside, the children were delighted with caring for the caterpillars each day, ensuring they had plenty of leaves to munch on and dropping water droplets on their bodies to keep them hydrated.

Slowly but surely, the caterpillars started their climb to the long twig that came with the kit. There they hung until they were fully engulfed in their cocoons. Six fat little bundles hung from the tree as the caterpillars inside made their transformations.

One afternoon after a short lesson about how the caterpillars would soon emerge from their cocoons as butterflies, the teacher released the children for free play. They could choose any activity around the classroom, from painting to blocks to books. But most were only interested in visiting their caterpillars. The teacher smiled at the sight of children huddled around the enclosure. After some time, however, she became alarmed at how long the children were there. She glanced over to see that the door to the enclosure was open, and several tiny hands and arms were inside. The teacher rushed over to intervene, but it was too late. The children had pulled the five of the six cocoons apart in their attempt to help the butterflies get free.

The look on the teacher's face turned somber, causing a student to ask her what was wrong. She carefully explained to the children that the five caterpillars they had "helped" by breaking them out would soon die. "Why?" the children cried. The teacher explained that the struggle to free itself from the cocoon is essential to the butterfly's future. As it presses against the constraint of the cocoon, it is sending blood to its wings and strengthening them for the difficult task of flying. Furthermore, when the butterfly emerges, it doesn't fly away immediately. It needs time hanging from the twig to dry its wings and practice flapping its wings. But helping the undeveloped butterflies, the children had robbed them of the essential struggle necessary to fly.

The final butterfly who had been untouched became an example to the children of the bliss of struggle. They were able to watch it poke one body part after another through the tiny holes it created. They kept their hands off the final butterfly, allowing it to struggle its way out of the cocoon and complete its last days on the twig, prepping for the next phase of life.

The day came to release the lone victorious butterfly who had managed to survive a classroom of youngsters. It was a grand and glorious event attended by students, teachers, and parents alike. This one little butterfly had taught everyone in the community the value of struggle. Thanks to its struggle, it broke loose from the branch and took to the wind. While its cohorts had fallen dead on the enclosure floor, its struggle had allowed it to finally fly free.

Humans could learn a lesson from that insect. The U.S., Canada, and other countries often assess high taxes with a plan to earmark billions of dollars for housing programs to address income inequality. In the U.S., for example, large housing developments are built as either single-family homes or high-rise apartment buildings. As an idea, it is genius. Provide housing for the poor at little to zero cost, allowing them an opportunity to save their funds to purchase a home of their own. But, in practice, it rarely succeeds. People living there complain of poor maintenance programs, ineffective pest control, and non-existent security. These housing communities quickly become havens of drugs, crime, and prostitution. The residents feel like they are in a war zone and expend their energy staying alive and keeping their families safe. Few ever escape to the paradise of homeownership. Lacking the struggle to provide for themselves and work toward buying a home, they remain stuck in the cycle of government housing for life. It is a failed experiment from the start since residents must be poor to enter the program. Once in, their income is reviewed yearly. If they are found to be making money above a certain threshold, they lose their housing voucher, defeating the program's purpose.

By contrast, another family might choose to reject government intervention and work together as a family toward one goal: saving enough for a down payment on a new home. It may take them three, five, or ten years to have enough to purchase their home. But there are no constraints on their income. They earn as much as they can, knowing that every dollar brings them closer to the ultimate goal. On the day they turn the lock on their new home, their sense of achievement overwhelms them. They are empowered to move toward bigger and better goals because they have proven to themselves that they can do it.

This is not, by any means, meant to be a political commentary on social welfare programs. It is simply an example of the blessing of struggling to achieve a goal rather than having some version of the goal handed out like Halloween candy. The point is that the struggles we face are powerful tools in our success, stemming from our ability to figure our way out of tough positions.

It has been said that if you give a man a fish, he eats for a day; teach a man to fish, he eats for a lifetime. While it is a beautiful saying, it should not be discounted that it is quite difficult to learn to fish. Fishing takes time. Fishing takes skill. Fishing takes bait. And even after the fish is caught, the task is not over. One must scale it, gut it, and cook it. Learning to fish is like all other things of value; they require effort. But the reward is lasting independence and a sense of accomplishment that money could never buy.

Chapter Five

Rough Starts

"There are different kinds of darkness," Rhys said… "There is the darkness that frightens, the darkness that soothes, the darkness that is restful." I pictured each. "There is the darkness of lovers and the darkness of assassins. It becomes what the bearer wishes it to be, needs it to be. It's not wholly bad or good."

~ Sarah J. Maas, A Court of Mist and Fury

Where you start is no indication of where you will finish. Whether it is a person, a company, or a country, a rough start might be just the thing to guarantee a strong finish. Starting from behind often causes people and entities to work harder and longer. They know that they are behind the eight ball. So, they give it their all just to catch up. And sometimes, they end up leading the pack.

Leonardo DiCaprio

Leonardo DiCaprio is an Oscar award-winning actor who has appeared in numerous films that have earned, all told, more than $7 billion and made him one of the top-grossing actors for many years. He can command $25 million for a starring role in a movie. When he is done with filming, he retires to his multimillion-dollar home. He even owns an island.

Despite his success and fame, he seems unspoiled by the trappings of Hollywood. He is considered fun to work with by actors, producers, and directors. He manages to keep his head out of the clouds and his feet firmly planted on the ground while being able to take on roles that run the gamut from the fabulously wealthy *Wolf of Wall Street,* to the poverty-stricken Jack Dawson in *Titanic.*

He credits his success in pictures, his range as an actor, and his down-to-earth demeanor to one thing: growing up poor. As a child in Los Angeles in the mid-1970s, his family struggled financially and moved from place to place around the city. However, wherever they landed, there was always prostitution and drugs along the city's streets. The streets nearly claimed him when he dropped out of high school before reaching his senior year.

FedEx

We all know FedEx as a global shipping giant with billions of dollars in revenue. But few people ever mention the fact that FedEx had a rough start. The company came out of the gate swinging but was immediately hit by the gas crisis of the 1970s. FedEx came so close to shutting down that they were left with just $5,000 in the bank.

Albert Einstein

Albert Einstein's name is synonymous with genius. He took the world of science and math by storm. But his start in education was almost his death knell. His teachers found him distracted and disruptive to other students. He had the words "mentally slow" plastered on his school record. His mother pulled him from the school so he could learn at home, unlocking his genius brain and passion for knowledge.

Walt Disney

Disney had a job as a cartoonist long before developing his own company. The owner of the company fired him because he "lacked imagination." Disney went on to create what might be the world's greatest and most well-known theme park and the character of Mickey Mouse.

J. K. Rowling

J. K. was a single parent receiving government assistance. Her mother had just died, and she was estranged from her father. She was riding a train when the idea of Harry Potter landed on her like a dove. She started writing the story when she got home because she didn't even have an ink pen with her at the time. That story became a billion-dollar franchise of movies, books, and theme parks.

Dolly Parton

Dolly has graced the greatest stages of the world. But it didn't start that way. She was raised in an old cabin deep in the woods with floors of nothing but dirt. Today, she is worth $500 million.

Airbnb

Nobody was interested in the fledgling business of Airbnb when it was founded. Multiple Silicon Valley investors passed when offered the opportunity to invest. Who would pay to sleep in someone's guest room, and who would allow strangers to spend the night in their home? It made no sense to anyone but the company's founder, who was living in a tiny apartment and surviving on cereal. But once the first rooms were sold, the idea took shape, then took off, making billions in revenue.

Reddit

When it started, Reddit was such a bust that it could not generate a single visitor. To bolster activity, the company's founder created accounts with fake names and started posting amongst themselves to give the site some traction. Today, it is one of the most popular sites online.

Oprah

Her name is a household word. It is known in every corner of the world today. But she started her life as an orphan in Mississippi. She was taken in by her grandmother and raped as a child. She gave birth to a baby that died. When she said she wanted to appear on TV, Oprah was discouraged by people who said she wasn't pretty enough. Today, she is a multibillionaire, having hosted one of TV's most successful shows in history.

Chapter Six

Taking Inventory

"Four be the things I am wiser to know:
Idleness, sorrow, a friend, and a foe.
Four be the things I'd been better without:
Love, curiosity, freckles, and doubt.
Three be the things I shall never attain:
Envy, content, and sufficient champagne.
Three be the things I shall have till I die:
Laughter and hope and a sock in the eye."

~ *Dorothy Parker,* The Complete Poems of Dorothy Parker

In a powerful biblical text, Moses, the leader of the Israelite people, has been tasked with moving more than a million people from Egypt to Canaan. Moses is not up for the task. He immediately launches into a flurry of complaints about what he lacked:

- I am too old.
- I don't speak well.
- I stutter.
- I have a criminal record.

Everything Moses said about himself was true. He was advancing in years. He had a wicked stutter that made him unintelligible at times. And he had murdered an Egyptian worker for whipping an Israelite slave.

Jehovah responds with a question, asking Moses what object he holds in his hand. I can imagine Moses looking down and seeing a weathered, wooden stick and wondering what God was referring to. Certainly, a repurposed branch, which Moses used as a staff, could not make up for all the ways in which he was deficient.

There is a crisis of creativity in our world that has led to a breakdown in people's ability to dream of something greater than the reality they are living. I could speculate on the source of the crisis that has all but killed our creativity. I could blame television, media, electronics, etc. But that is not a useful exercise. How we got here is not as important as where we go from here.

Let's step back in time and recall a season in your life when you were highly creative. You could make fun in almost any environment. A long car ride became an opportunity to explore the passing cars and count the red ones while your sibling counted the blue ones. You rejoiced when you were declared the winner! You might remember opening your presents on your birthday or at Christmas and playing with each one before taking the boxes and making a small city complete with a general store, a doctor's office, and a supermarket. Your neurons were constantly firing. While you slept, you dreamed vividly of things you had never seen before, causing your parents to wonder how you could have dreamed of them. You made friends so easily that you could connect with another kid within seconds and be off together on some adventure. Your sense of exploration caused you to investigate everything around you to see what it was and how it worked.

Creativity was your life, and your life was being creative. Now tell me... when did you lose that? When did you become stuffy and serious? When did life lose its verve and spark and just become some dreaded routine you repeated day after day? When did a two-week vacation become the highlight of your year? When did you trade the wonder, imagination, and discovery life handed you at birth for a safe job, cookie-cutter house, and ironic SUV? I'll bet you don't know the date because it was a slow death of the creative you and the gradual replacement of the more responsible, but less happy, you.

So, you read books like this hoping for either information or inspiration that will break the vicious cycle and connect your dreams to your reality sometime between now and dead!

I had an advantage in making this transformation. Being born in poverty was a tremendous blessing in that it placed me on the bottom with few places to go but up. Going any further down would have meant addiction, homelessness, or death. I passed on those options. I looked up until I could get up. And I used my creativity like Moses' staff to lean on.

What's in your hand? What do you have that you have not considered, that you have overlooked, or that you have discounted? Where does your personal magic lie?

Life asks a critical and very complex question we seek to answer: How do I live my best life? How do we squeeze every drop out of our lives to ensure that we reach our final days in peace, knowing we did what we could and that we did *all* we could?

It is a question that people have asked themselves and others for generations. From the sage gurus to the neighborhood plumber, we are all trying to find meaning in the mundane. Religion seeks to answer. Philosophy seeks to answer. Even your barber or hairstylist might have taken a crack at it. Some of the responses we come up with are actually quite good and seem to come close to feeling like the right answer.

Some believe that living your best life is all about pushing yourself to higher and higher levels of achievement. They think that we get bored with the ordinary and require a challenge to feel purposeful and fulfilled. They suggest we must maximize the moments of our life since we are merely mortal and have a finite amount of time on the earth. They are not wrong. Accumulating experiences can and will add depth to your life. We will cover quite a bit about that in a later chapter.

Others use terms like discovering your bliss. They suggest that we are all "burdened with glorious purpose" and must do that one thing. Life, they say, is all about the quest to find that true calling and then figure out how to live for that calling each day. They suggest that freedom and happiness can only be found when we maximize that unique calling that is tied to our purpose. Without clear purpose, they would say, life feels shallow and meaningless. I would tend to agree with that crowd as well. There truly is no substitute for having a clear direction.

However, others approach this from a completely different perspective. They warn against the dangers of setting lofty goals tied to money or business or travel as it might lead to a trap where life becomes an accumulation of material possessions. They would caution us that the desire for fame, success, wealth, adventure, etc., carries inherent dangers. Not the least of which is the likelihood that we will become like the hamster stuck on the wheel of life who is always in pursuit and never attains. They would recommend that life's ultimate goals should be to discover inner peace and pursue a life of gratitude. They would tell us to live more simply and slowly to savor all of the gifts we have been given as people. It's the "stop long enough to smell the roses" approach to living.

This begs the question: who is right? The answer may be that they are all correct in their own way. It does not come down to an "either-or" choice but a "both-and" choice.

I've been fortunate in my life to meet lots of people and have many experiences. I have known people who gambled with their personal potential and lost big. I have also witnessed people who have reached the highest levels of achievement and success only to confess that they felt lost and empty. I have been a keen observer of it all and have come away with this… People who understand the darkness fare better in the light.

What I mean is that it is hard to come from privilege and still experience the thrill that comes from overcoming the odds. There are very few odds to overcome. But when someone has come from nothing or has lost everything and gained it back, they have a special appreciation for life.

The differences are not really the approach to life, but rest in each individual's perspective. Perhaps you, like me, have listened to an interview of a very successful person in the field of sports, politics, entertainment, etc. The interviewer often asks, "What is the secret to your success?" Perhaps you moved closer to the edge of your seat to hear what that person might say was the element that clinched it for them. But then their answer was simple, boring, and completely underwhelming, almost as if they did not know the secret to their success at all.

When they revealed their big "secret," you might have sat back in your seat and said, "That's it?" If I were asked that question today, my answer would be clear. The secret to my success is my failure. It was the death blows I was dealt during the formative years. The teenage years weren't much better. It was like a continuing onslaught that I experienced over many years. I was beaten so low that I had nowhere to go but up.

Perhaps you find that disturbing, disappointing, or demotivating. You might wonder why suffering and struggle are a part of the success secret. But please allow me to shift your thinking and challenge you to consider the possibility that the experiences you most abhor are the ones that built character in you. The difficulties you don't like to discuss are the ones that made you strong.

You may have heard an interesting story about a man who left his home on a journey to find diamonds. He traveled in and around Africa for years, searching for diamonds. He invested his life savings into the quest. After years of searching, however, he could not uncover even a single diamond field. He finally gave up and returned home, despondent and dejected. He had only enough money to purchase his plane ticket back to his humble farm. He decided to till his own land to plant seeds to grow enough food to feed himself. He spent the rest of his days in despair that he was never able to find diamonds. After his death, his land was sold. The person who bought his land dug just a few feet beyond the man's little garden and found diamonds. They were there with him in his own backyard the entire time.

Your story of pain, loss, abandonment, disillusionment, or failure is your diamond field. It shouldn't be hidden. It should be shared. In our failure, we can relate to those trying to reach their goals.

This theme is repeated in all great literature, from the first books printed down to this one. If we look at literature from an honest perspective, we must admit that there are really no new stories. All of the stories are essentially the same. They all start out identically: man is on a quest, man braves the dangers to reach the destination, man finds that what he is looking for is not the thing he searched for in the first place, and man discovers that he already had what he was searching for. We see it in Pinocchio, Cinderella, even in the story of the Jews search for the Messiah. It has always been and will always be that the power over life and death rests within reach—just over a fine line. That should be seen as good news. It means that you do not need permission to be successful. You do not need to be born into riches or nobility. You do not even need high levels of intelligence or knowledge. Your wealthy place (however you choose to define it) has already been wired into your DNA. You simply need to take the journey, not to some foreign land, but into your own soul and psyche to find it.

The journey is still a critical part of the process. All aspects of the journey matter, not just the happily ever after at the end. You must be able to recognize and acknowledge that what you have been through makes a difference in where you are today. It didn't break you. It helped to make you.

Have you ever seen brilliant people who don't think they are that intelligent? Or beautiful people who think they are average-looking? Or rich people who claim they don't have a lot of money? We are notoriously flawed at taking inventory of our lives accurately enough to assess what about us makes us so unique. And we are often surrounded by people who see our special qualities and never mention them to us or, worse, who ridicule us about the ways we are different. The truth is that everybody is different. We are unique, weird, quirky, and peculiar. Some of us are just better at suppressing it than others. Kudos to the weirdos!

Chapter Seven

The Comfy Trap

"I have realized; it is during the times I am far outside my element that I experience myself the most. That I see and feel who I really am the most! I think that's what a comet is like, you see, a comet is born in the outer realms of the universe! But it's only when it ventures too close to our sun or to other stars that it releases the blazing "tail" behind it and shoots brazen through the heavens! And meteors become sucked into our atmosphere before they burst like firecrackers and realize that they're shooting stars! That's why I enjoy taking myself out of my own element, my own comfort zone, and hurling myself out into the unknown. Because it's during those scary moments, those unsure steps taken, that I am able to see that I'm like a comet hitting a new atmosphere: suddenly I illuminate magnificently, and fire dusts begin to fall off of me! I discover a smile I didn't know I had, I uncover a feeling that I didn't know existed in me... I see myself. I'm a shooting star. A meteor shower. But I'm not going to die out... like a comet... I'm just going to keep on coming back."
~ C. JoyBell C.

You probably have a good life, all things considered. Statistically, if you had enough disposable income to buy this book, you are among the millions of us who are living well, comparatively speaking. The cost of this book, in some cultures, will feed a family for a week. So, the fact that you don't have a leer jet, a Blohm and Vass yacht, or a $40,000 Rolex is not an indicator of your wealth on the worldwide spectrum. According to Credit Suisse, just $4,000 in money or assets makes you wealthier than half of the world's population. It's fun to throw jabs at the "one percent" of the world's wealth holders. But, riches aside, you are likely among the ten percent of the world's population who hold about eighty-five percent of the remaining wealth. But you already know that, and that stat might have been impactful to you the first time you heard it. But now, you probably gloss over it as you call the bank to raise the limit on your credit card.

The point is that most of us are quite comfortable. And where we generally experience discomfort is when we are seeking to add to our wealth or material possessions. I understand. I face the trap of comfortability just like you do. I live in a lovely home and have enough money to last long beyond my death. I am surrounded by loving family and friends. What more could anyone want? Comfort seems like a great goal to obtain.

An old saying calls such a state "sheep in the dry" and refers to the state where the shepherd has plenty of sheep to start the next season when it comes. The shepherd is sitting pretty, knowing that there will be plenty of wool and a handsome profit for the shepherd to enjoy. That is where I am in my life — a very comfortable situation. It is a far cry from the threadbare childhood I experienced early in life.

But having "sheep in the dry" comes with some dangerous side effects. These are the curses of comfort:

- Comfort thwarts creativity.
- Comfort breeds laziness.
- Comfort rejects challenge.

You've heard the stories of actors who make their way to Hollywood and then barely survive on the income from waiting tables while they audition for part after part. Or perhaps you have heard the story of some industrial tycoon whose early days were spent sleeping in the office of his factory because he could no longer afford his mortgage. Those tough beginnings wrung out of them the creativity that caused them to ultimately have success.

I am reminded of the Alibaba founder and CEO. He was born in the bottom class of China to parents who were trying to scrape by as musicians. Then KFC opened its first chain in China. Jack worked hard to learn English by giving away free tours of China to English-speaking tourists to practice the language. He applied for one of the twenty-three open positions. Twenty-four people applied, but he was the only one who was not offered a position.

He went to college to study English and worked as a teacher for $12 per month. After several attempts to get into Harvard and just as many rejections, he came to the U.S. to learn computers. He convinced a group of friends to invest in this wild idea for a company that provided low prices on quality goods. Thus, Alibaba was born. It was headquartered in Jack's tiny apartment, but grew to be the largest company in China and one of the largest in the world.

Now, roll back the tape and imagine what would have happened if Jack had accomplished his goal of getting a job at KFC. He would have been making more money than any kid his age in his poor community. He would have rejoiced. But he would also have been lured into a mediocre life. However, if he had not failed, if he didn't have to struggle, and if he had not been rejected, he might have learned to settle for a safe life.

"We keep fighting. We keep changing ourselves. We don't complain. Never give up. Today is hard, tomorrow will be worse, but the day after tomorrow will be sunshine."

~ Jack Ma

***

We think we want comfort, but if we play out a life of extreme comfort with no unmanageable challenges to its logical conclusion, we would find life deadly dull. Our hearts break when we see news reports of fires, floods, hurricanes, and other disasters. We weep for the dead and contribute to the charities that support the survivors. In our hearts, though, we wish we could have spared them the tragedy.

But imagine if you could. What would happen? In a world where there is no sickness, death, or tragedy, what would be the place of compassion, care, and service? What would life offer to satisfy our need to solve problems? How would we show our care and concern for others?

You can see it in your own life. The ebb and flow of good times and bad make life worth living. Without adversity, you feel you are not alive anymore, and you start dying. You can prove this is true by thinking about what happens on a long vacation or holiday. When you arrive at your vacation destination, you are thrilled to be away from the hustle and bustle. You are happy to be in a place where no chores are waiting to be done, and the phone does not ring every other minute. You turn off your notifications and let the world attempt to survive without you.

However, as the days wear on, leisure itself becomes a chore. Laying in bed watching movies becomes unbearable. Being a tourist is great for the first few days, but even that does not satisfy.

You were never meant to be static. You are constantly growing and changing. You either grow up or down. I think there is not much in between.

More and more seniors are choosing not to retire. Some need the money. But a growing segment of seniors is choosing to skip retirement even though they are financially set.

Rodney Brooks of U.S. News and World Report explains this growing trend:

It's not uncommon for baby boomers to continue to work well into their 60s, 70s, or even 80s... With continued improvements in health care and life expectancy, people can spend as long in retirement as they spent working.

Here are the top reasons not to retire:
- *Find fulfillment in an organization's work.*
- *Improve your retirement finances.*
- *Continue to support worthy causes.*
- *Stay engaged and mentally sharp.*

Clint Camua, Vice President of EP Wealth Advisors in West Los Angeles, says one of his clients worked into her early 80s at two different jobs, even though she didn't need the money. "She worked as an assistant to a judge from 7 a.m. to 3 or 4 p.m. Then, she would go to the racetrack and be a security guard, carrying a weapon."

Sandra McPeak, Managing Director of Investments at Wells Fargo Advisors, says many people follow a nontraditional path to retirement or even unretire. "A lot of times, people, when they retire, think they will have all this time. They think they can catch up," McPeak says. "But after a while, they are drumming their fingers. They feel out of it. They don't feel engaged. They feel like they aren't contributing." But there's no need to give up on a profession you love just because you reach a certain age.

George Fraser, a noted public speaker, author, and networking expert, has never tried to retire and has no intention of doing so. "I enjoy my work more than vacation. I'm not a sit at the beach and chill kind of guy," Fraser says. "I'll either die sitting at a podium or at my desk dotting an 'i' or crossing a 't.'"

Fraser says he can't imagine himself in retirement and has no close friends who are retired. "If your health allows you, don't ever retire," Fraser says. "If your work enthralls you and excites you, you should keep doing it until your last breath. It will keep you interested and engaged with life. It'll keep you curious."

***

To escape the comfy trap, you must decide to challenge yourself in ways you never have. Just as the bodybuilder gains muscle by lifting heavier weights, you must build your muscle. I'm always looking for new challenges. And while my wife sometimes balks at some new obligation, trip, or contraption in the house, by keeping myself open to new experiences, I keep my spirit of adventure fresh and alive.

When my business went broke in the 90s, I didn't curl up in the corner feeling depressed. I was resilient. I knew that I would make a strong comeback. Sure enough, I stayed strong, and the business came roaring back.

For example, I owned several successful advertising companies. I reached a place where I had achieved all I wanted to accomplish in that business. It was time for a new risk. I could have easily rested on my laurels and trusted that my current book of reliable customers would keep coming back. It would have been comfortable. But it would have also been boring. What I would have gained in reliable income I would have lost in zeal, energy, and challenges for my mind. So, I sold those businesses.

Once the sale was consummated, it was not the time for me to kick back and count my spoils. I immediately started a new company — publishing magazines in and around Europe. After some time publishing, I again realized that I was getting far too comfortable. Coronavirus hit Austria, sparking a wave of mandatory lockdowns across Europe. So, I looked for other opportunities.

Since the entire world was sheltering in place, I decided it would be an excellent opportunity to become a student again. And for me, it was a great chance to study the many things that had interested me for years but which I had placed on the back burner. No one knew how long the lockdowns would last, but I did not want to waste a moment. I enrolled in school and became the oldest student in Switzerland, studying hypnotherapy and meditation.

Since I couldn't be out in the world opening businesses and running them, I decided to invest in businesses in this vein of mindfulness. At the time, my daughter had founded a very large studio for modern spirituality. It seemed like a perfect chance for me to get involved in the industry in a meaningful way.

Then, I began to look at all of the notes I had accumulated over the years — just bits and pieces of knowledge and wisdom I had acquired. So, I decided to start writing books to share what I have learned and my experiences with as many people as possible.

For me, the coronavirus pandemic was like pushing the stop button on time. It gave me time to reflect and retool. It offered me a chance to go to school when I could focus all of my time and energy. It presented new business investment avenues. And it allowed me to spend more time with my daughter in the opening of a mindfulness studio. I found time to write and search for new challenges.

I am painfully aware that the pandemic cost many people their lives or the lives of loved ones. I am sympathetic to their loss. At the same time, I am thankful for the blessings.

Coronavirus brought the entire world to slow down. It gave the air a chance to recover from the relentless carbon emissions. It gave animals a chance to replenish from hunting and fishing. It gave people an opportunity to spend time with those they loved. Did you seize the lockdown of 2020 and 2021? Or did you waste it worrying and complaining?

This is the message I trust every reader will get: your life has a purpose. No matter what has happened in your past, regardless of where you started in life, and no matter what obstacles you are currently facing, that purpose never dissolves.

Dreams never die. They only grow more silent. When you are young, your dreams are screaming at you day and night to pay attention to them. If you ignore them in your youth, they may stop screaming, but they continue to speak, hoping you will listen. If you ignore them in adulthood, they speak even more softly, but they do speak. When you reach old age, your ignored dreams remain with you as a whisper. You feel it as regret — regret for the things you didn't try, regret over the missed chances, and regret for the excuses you made not to do the things you felt compelled to do.

The good news is that if you respond to the call of your dreams, they will always speak loudly and clearly. You could be 50, 60, 70, or 80. Your dreams know that when they speak, you will respond. Never be afraid to listen and act on those deep desires of your heart. No matter the outcome, you will be thankful you did.

Live! Don't just breathe. Don't just exist. Live! Listen carefully to your inner conversation. Are you routinely responding to your heart's desire with a list of reasons why you can't do this or that?

- I'm too old.
- I'm too young.
- I'm not educated enough.
- I don't have enough money.
- People might judge me if I do that.

Understand that you can do whatever you want. You are free. The world is out there, and it is waiting for you to explore all that it has to offer. This is the greatest time in history. You could not have been born in a time more suited for taking risks and exploring your options. In the 17th century, it would take more than two months to sail from England to the United States. Today, you can fly from London to New York in 8 hours. Access to technology means you can start a thriving business without even owning or leasing a building. You can conference with people in Africa, Asia, Europe, the U.S., and everywhere else in the world using a handheld device that fits in your pocket.

Resilience and tenacity are the names of the game, no matter what era you are born into. These are lessons I learned early in life. The people who kept trying eventually succeeded. Those who gave up succumbed to alcoholism, poverty, or suicide because times were so hard. This lesson of resilience is the key to any adversity life throws your way.

WDSU Television Station in Australia aired the story of Nick Vujicic. Nick is ordinary in most ways. He is married. He has four children. He has a great career. He enjoys boating and a host of other hobbies. What is extraordinary about Nick is what he doesn't have: arms or legs.

Nick Vujicic has a passion for sharing his story across the globe. He was born in Australia without arms and legs with no medical explanation. He said he had wanted to give up on life at age ten and attempted suicide.

"I didn't believe I'd get a job or get married and thought even if I got married, I can't even hold my wife's hand," said Vujicic.

But he says God helped him overcome all those obstacles. He even got married and is blessed with four beautiful children. Vujicic said he is living life without limits, on the ski slopes, and in the water. He enjoys many activities that may seem impossible, like swimming, golfing, and fishing.

He has taken his powerful story worldwide to 74 countries, 21 presidents, and ten government leaders. He wants to encourage the people of Southeast Louisiana never to give up and live with purpose regardless of the situation.

"Sometimes we wait for a miracle, but sometimes God wants to use us as a miracle even if we don't get ours," said Vujicic.

***

What is your excuse? There are none. Seize every opportunity.

When you become older, you may find yourself getting a little bit lazy or resting on your laurels. This is especially true for people who have earned enough money to live on. They have big pensions or other investments that have made them comfortable. They mistakenly think that this is the time for them to do nothing and "enjoy life." But often, their minds start to wither, as do their bodies. Before long, they are spending more time at the doctors' office than on the beaches.

Do not allow your life to fall into a state of atrophy. Get busy. Start walking, biking, or getting involved in sports. Paint, write books, or build models. Just because your birth certificate reveals your age, your body doesn't have to. You will feel younger and, as a result, look more youthful. If you are older, I assure you that the game is not over. It has just begun. You have the advantage of knowledge, wisdom, experience, and time!

Modern medicine allows us to live longer than ever. And longer life expectancy these days comes with real quality of life. You have to carry on doing the things you love. I don't advocate mindless activities. If you don't get a thrill from it, don't do it. Don't waste your days assembling puzzles if you don't love puzzles. Do something you find meaningful and challenging. If money is no object, this might be a great time to give back.

Chapter Eight

The Dreaded Comfort Zone

Hard times create strong men.
Strong men create good times.
Good times create weak men.
And, weak men create hard times.
~ G. Michael Hopf

Part of your affection for the comfort zone is not your fault. We are hardwired in both our physiology and psychology to live in our comfort zone. Without a comfort zone, life would be wholly unbearable. We would find it impossible to function day-to-day and would live in a heightened state of fear and terror. Our comfort zones allow us to have familiar surroundings, familiar friends, and familiar experiences. These keep us grounded in the world.

However, we are not designed to maintain the type of sameness and lack of adventure many of us experience daily. We are supposed to have a balance of calm vs. excitement, familiarity vs. strangeness, tranquility vs. opposition. The body needs it, as does the mind.

Our affinity for our comfort zones arises out of something called homeostasis. It is best understood by looking at the body's systems and how they work nonstop to keep us alive. Let's take your temperature, which must remain somewhere close to 98.6 degrees Fahrenheit. That is true for people in most places, even the coldest places on earth, like Alaska and Siberia. The body can handle slight fluctuations in that core temperature. Anything between 97 and 99 would not raise any doctor's alarms. The body works day and night to maintain that temperature. If you get a little hot, the body automatically knows to sweat to cool you down. If you get a little cold, it knows that it must shiver to warm you up. All of this happens involuntarily. That's homeostasis.

However, just above 99 is where the danger starts. The body can only handle a few degrees above that optimal measurement before serious harm can be done. Immediately, the body goes into fever mode and sends signals everywhere that the danger of death is imminent. The same is true if the body drops below 97. It will coalesce all of its forces around the internal organs and sacrifice extremities like fingers, toes, arms, and legs to keep itself alive.

Homeostasis is at work in all of your natural systems. It regulates your blood pressure, water levels, sodium levels, and many other functions of the body. In the time it took you to read this sentence, your body's system forced you to breathe around three times without needing you to make it do so.

But there is also homeostasis of the mind. With this type of homeostasis, we want things to remain the same around us. We want to feel secure in our environment. Our brains seem to vacillate between needing stimulation and demanding consistency.

There is a constant dynamic tension between homeostasis and creative change. Too much change at once can disrupt internal balance. Too little change can lead to stagnation. With the media impact of endless stories of disasters and difficulties, we may develop a habitual tendency to focus on homeostasis, pulling back from creative change. We may find ourselves wishing our lives to be predictable, solid, and unchanging. If we forget the critical balance between the two systems and attempt to organize our lives to minimize change, we can profoundly limit both the possibilities for growth and satisfaction in our lives and our ability to respond to injury and illness when they happen.

~ Alison Bonds Shapiro, M.B.A., Psychology Today

***

The comfort zone we live in, though, has changed drastically over time. The last 100 years have been an exceptional time of great change. More has changed in the past 100 years, arguably, than in the 1,000 years before.

Our primitive brains are wired for consistency, but some of us seem to always seek change. Think back to what it might have been like for early mankind. It was eat or be eaten. Everything "out there" wanted to consume them. They lived under the constant threat of wild animals, unpredictable weather, and food that could potentially poison them. The best way to stay safe was to remain in the bosom of the community. Together, they were safer and stronger. Still, some people always felt an irresistible desire to venture out away from the group. They longed to know what was on the other side of the mountain or just beyond the trees. They went out there and explored.

Some of them never returned, but the ones who did could tell the rest of the community that there was food or water on the other side of the ridge. Because of their bravery and spirit of exploration, the whole community benefitted.

We don't have the same physical challenges today. Most of the surface of the earth has been explored. So, we continue to look for new ways to push ourselves. Unlike our ancestors, we struggle to find new ways to accomplish this because life is so good.

Thinking about the world from a historical perspective, before 2020, you would have to admit the world was experiencing a period of "good times." Of course, the phrase "good times" is extremely relative since there are always troublesome events around the world, and there will always be. Life is never easy. It is always marked by suffering in one way or another. But, in general, with all things considered, most would likely agree with the suggestion that pre-2020 should be classified as the good times.

One hundred years ago, the world was at war. Poverty was rampant in all undeveloped nations. Even a mild sickness could mean death. And without sickness, people were still likely to die sometime around or just after their 40th birthdays. A pandemic like COVID-19 could easily have wiped out a billion people rather than the 5.63 million lives it took so far. The Spanish flu proved it by killing 120 million over the space of about two years.

But in 2020 and the era just preceding it, economies were growing more robust in more places worldwide than ever before. The global poverty rate dropped from 10.5 percent to

9.2 percent, indicating that more people were clawing their way out of abject poverty than the year before. There were no hot wars in the world, though incursions remained as they always will. The global life expectancy was also climbing dramatically. The fastest-growing economies in the world were found in India, Asia, and sub-Saharan Africa, places where suffering, arguably, has been the worst historically.

Certainly, the working class in the western world had more access to quality food, electronics, and cars. Homes got bigger and more people got homes. It would be hard to argue against the idea that the world before COVID-19 and in the last decade or so was relatively good.

However, the problem with good times is that they lead to a kind of weakness that, over time, produces weak minds and feeble wills. Weakness of thought, action, spirit, etc., makes the entire world vulnerable. As we grow more and more sophisticated as a technological society, we are required to do less and less on our own.

One could argue that it was a chore to wash our own clothes, chop our own firewood, and grow our own food. But the counterargument could also be made that the generations who were able to do that were much more resilient and self-sufficient.

In February of 2021, while the world was still struggling with the coronavirus pandemic, eastern Texas in the United States was hit with temperatures below zero. For a state that is primarily desert climates and enjoys triple-digit temperatures in the summertime, it is fair to say the residents living in that area were ill-prepared for the deep freeze. No one knew what to do to keep themselves warm amid the subzero weather, which was also marked by ice and snow. Homes had not been built with insulation or proper plumbing systems to withstand such temperatures. Then, the power grid failed, leaving millions in the dark with no heat. The terrible weather lasted for days. It was the coldest storm in fifty years. Hundreds of people died. A child froze to death as he slept in his cold bedroom. It was a horrifying scene.

In response to the crisis, Texas and U.S. officials took a close look at the power grid since it could not withstand the cold weather and reached such catastrophic levels. As it turns out, it was four minutes away from completely collapsing. Texans complained that the grid was not hardened and was ill-prepared for any sort of weather crisis. Was it a foreseeable event? Some say yes. After all, though Texas is one of the warmest states in the U.S., it is not uncommon for winter months to fall below freezing. But there was another complicating factor. Texas had been growing in popularity and had become known as a place where taxes were low and freedom was high. More than four million people had relocated to the state in the preceding years, placing additional strain on the power grid. So, it seems that officials and power companies might have predicted a need to upgrade their infrastructure. But what about its citizens?

Had this crisis happened one hundred years earlier, it would have hardly been a blip on the radar. In fact, records indicate a similar cold snap just fifty years ago, which swept through the same area, delivering similar frigid temperatures—and the residents managed it quite well. Why? Almost everyone knew how to chop firewood, and many of the homes had fireplaces. But in 2020, people who had fireplaces used them more for decoration than their intended function. Fireplaces were where they hung stockings at Christmastime.

It was not uncommon for cold weather to pass through central and eastern Texas. It just didn't usually stay very long. This time, it lingered. But it revealed that people had none of the emergency supplies all people everywhere should have:

- Stored food
- Extra water
- Cash
- Extra medications
- Backup power supply
- Alternative heating source

People could have lasted twice as long without much trouble with those basics. One might think it was poor Texans who suffered the most. But footage showed high-dollar neighborhoods with price tags in the mid-six-figure range where the residents moved into their cars to stay warm and gave interviews demanding that the government bring water to their homes. This is the modern mindset. People have been made comfortable by the easy availability of food and other necessities, never thinking they may have to take care of themselves.

This is not the comfort zone we should aspire to. In fact, this kind of comfort zone leaves people stranded praying for help.

The bliss of struggle occurs when you are trained to leave your comfort zone intentionally. You step away from the comforts and luxuries you have enjoyed and push yourself to do what you would not ordinarily do. That is exactly what makes you strong and resilient.

A person who was born with the golden spoon is, in reality, quite poor because, if you remove the spoon, he loses everything. Think back to the stock market crash of 1929. A run on the banks forced them to close. People in London were the first to notice the financial meltdown. Then word hit New York. And for the next ten years, the West struggled through the crisis. Though people didn't jump off tall buildings in droves as the myth suggests, the suicide rate exploded in response to the lost wealth of so many. Some people gassed themselves, others set themselves on fire, and others swallowed poison because they had lost their money. Many who remained alive resorted to begging for food and money on the streets.

How could the biggest financial boom in history at the time be followed so suddenly by the biggest downturn? And why would the reaction of the financial world be so drastic? Good times create weakness. In good times, we relax and fail to take the precautions needed to survive. In good times, we have little opportunity to exercise the virtues that make life good—like courage. We live as little kings of our own tiny kingdoms. We can be easily warmed and cooled and refuse to tolerate the slightest variation. Our food is readily available, sparing us the time or bother of hunting it, killing it, dressing it, and storing it. Our televisions have gotten bigger as our muscles grow smaller.

Speaking of television, every possible entertainment need we may have is easily met, making it more challenging to blast us out of our homes to enjoy a night out. For that reason, symphony subscriptions are declining faster than anyone ever imagined possible. The same is true of other art forms that must be enjoyed in person, like the theater, museums, and dance performances. Libraries are all but empty, with the exception of the free computer stations.

New York Times writer Anthony Tomassine caught up to the President of the Los Angeles Philharmonic, Deborah Borda, to discuss the disappearing subscription base:

…Things were going well for the orchestra, Ms. Borda said, except for one challenge facing ensembles everywhere: the steady decline of concertgoers who buy their tickets through subscriptions.

This was hardly news. But the shift has been stark and the figures troubling. Ms. Borda, one of the most innovative arts administrators in the business, said that within her institution, everyone has been operating under the assumption that subscriptions will essentially be gone in ten years.

…The shrinkage of the subscription base has undoubtedly upset the status quo. America's orchestras and opera companies counted on subscribers to fill their halls for generations. And plenty of people were willing to sign up, especially orchestra fans, who got into the habit of spending every Thursday, or every other Saturday, at the symphony mingling with other regulars.

But today, when most people, and not just young ones, are accustomed to choosing their own times and devices for watching television shows and movies or listening to music, the idea of committing yourself to a regularly scheduled night at your local orchestra hall can seem antiquated, even to hear a particular program you're very interested in.

***

Even the premier orchestras have suffered from the effects of the cushy life. The New York Philharmonic routinely sold more than eighty percent of ticket sales through their subscription program. Today, just over half their tickets were sold through subscription, putting the future of the orchestra at risk.

Yet this downward spiral could be salutary if it forces classical ensembles to rethink the standard seasonal format, in which a program is repeated three or four times in the course of a week. With subscribers fleeing, orchestras might be more willing to devote larger chunks of the calendar to mini-festivals offering an array of one-time programs linked to an overall theme. And special projects like the Philharmonic's hugely popular production of Stephen Sondheim's "Sweeney Todd" last season might be scheduled for an extended run.

***

It's not just the fine and performing arts affected by a society more interested in their cell phones than the cello. It seems we are also failing to raise a generation of youth who want to make the years-long commitment to learning to play an instrument. Why should they when 100 apps will have you playing Chopin in minutes via a video game?

In May 2020, a Toronto paper discovered that Indiana State University had discarded tens of thousands of dollars worth of pianos in the dumpsters behind the school. When the story broke, the assumption was that the pianos were old or broken. But an investigative reporter revealed that many of the pianos, tossed nose-first into the trash, were in good working order. Piano technician, Dean May, was asked to inspect the pianos. He said:

"I thought I'll just swing by and take a look at the dumpsters to see what I found, and I was just stunned and shocked. I could tell by observing that this was a high-end piano. It looked to be in excellent condition. The strings didn't have any tarnish on them, the soundboard was good, the finish, what hadn't been destroyed, was good. My technician friend told me that these pianos all came out of the music department, not out of dormitories, so they were all reasonably maintained."

***

Students spent less time learning to play piano and more time in the computer lab designing video games or shooting videos to upload to social media. Gone were the days when the music hall was filled with the sounds of dozens of piano rooms where students perfected their craft.

When the school president was asked about the waste, he admitted that no one was interested in the pianos. They listed them for auction online and fetched bids no higher than $25. Local schools and other organizations declined when they attempted to donate the pianos.

This is not just a fist shake at modern technology and the state of the younger generation. Every generation has complained about its youth, usually to no avail.

"Many [young people] were so pampered nowadays that they had forgotten that there was such a thing as walking, and they made automatically for the buses… unless they did something, the future for walking was very poor indeed."
Scottish Rights of Way: More Young People Should Use Them, Falkirk Herald, 1951

***

"Parents themselves were often the cause of many difficulties. They frequently failed in their obvious duty to teach self-control and discipline to their own children."
Problems of Young People, Leeds Mercury, 1938

***

"We defy anyone who goes about with his eyes open to deny that there is, as never before, an attitude on the part of young folk which is best described as grossly thoughtless, rude, and utterly selfish."
The Conduct of Young People, Hull Daily Mail, 1925

***

It's strange to hear of people one hundred years ago complaining that their youth are spoiled and lazy. But the issue today is far more concerning. In the past, youth may not have lived up to their parents' expectations. They might have appeared to be as spoiled and lazy as the youth of today seem to be. However, the big difference in the 21st century is that our youth are laboring under a sense of real despair, despite living in the greatest era of all humankind.

As William Hasseltine wrote for Forbes Magazine:

A CDC online survey indicates that young people between the ages of 18-24 are more likely to suffer mental health problems during the pandemic than any age group.

According to this survey, 63% of young people are suffering significant symptoms of anxiety or depression. Nearly a quarter of respondents reported that they had started or increased their abuse of substances, including alcohol, marijuana, and prescription drugs, to cope with their emotions... This data quantifies an alarming trend that we have seen emerge anecdotally, that the pandemic will have a long-lasting impact on young people's mental health.

For young people navigating choices about higher education, their careers, building relationships, or deciding when to start a family, the uncertainty of the pandemic can add pressure to already stressful decisions... The study highlighted the rising trend in loneliness among young adults compared to the elderly. As discussed, loneliness is at the root of many mental health issues. In a national survey of approximately 950 Americans, 36 percent reported feeling lonely "frequently" or "almost all the time" in the past four weeks. Sixty-one percent of the respondents aged 18 to 25 reported high levels of loneliness.

***

Struggles

No matter how much it hurts now, someday you will look back and realize your struggles changed your life for the better.

Chapter Nine

Sheep in the Dry

"We are not rich by what we possess but by what we can do without."
~ Immanuel Kant

For me, there is no need to work for money anymore. I am financially secure for the rest of my life, even if I live past a hundred. But that does not mean my work is over. In fact, it has just begun. I help my mayor in Kitzbühel, Austria. I share my thoughts through writing books. And I give talks to help people discover their inner strength through hypnotherapy. I also help people to go into the publishing business.

I work as hard now as I ever did in the early days when we struggled. I will never forget those times. They remain precious to me. I had a wife, and we had two kids. We were not wealthy at that time. In fact, we had literally no money. It was a crazy life consumed with making ends meet while trying to seize opportunities to better our situation. I remember feeling the dark clouds of poverty gathering over my head, changing my emotional atmospheric pressure. But, while I was there at the bottom, feeling blue, I would say to myself, "Come on! Things will turn around." I had no evidence on which to base my belief other than the words themselves. I would start some venture and then watch it crash and burn. With the smoke of the last failure still on my clothes and the scars on my soul fresh and new, I would just try again. Again and again, I threw my heart and soul at whatever endeavor I was pursuing. Finally, I tried, and it worked out.

The blessing of poverty, pain, loss, suffering, etc., was that it left me with no other choice but to succeed. For the wealthy, every move they make is filled with risk. Poverty removes the financial risk. You have nothing — so you have nothing to lose. I think poverty can be quite beautiful. It was wonderful to watch the world around me change as I grew, learned, and earned.

When I watch documentaries about poor villages, I rarely see anyone sitting around doing nothing. These are busy little communities. Everyone has their role, and each person plays this role to perfection. They rely on each other to complete their tasks. This life is all that they have ever known. They do not fret about their own car's age compared to the neighbor's newer car.

I call it the poverty effect. These people do not measure life in dollars or pounds. They do not measure their worth by their meaningless possessions. So, it begs the question, what is poverty?

Poverty can show itself in many ways beyond the number of digits in your bank balance. There is poverty of mind; poverty of love; poverty of spirit; and poverty of knowledge. These communities that many look down on because of the way they live may have a higher happiness index than those living in the finest communities around the world. While middle-class people (who are actually wealthy) are sitting around with the television remote in their hands complaining that they are bored, these undeveloped communities are busy working. If you compare one group to the other, it is hard to deny that the poor community is the one that is really alive.

They don't feel really poverty in the ways we do. In reality, they enjoy a kind of wealth most communities in Europe and the U.S. have lost sight of. They have wealth of community, wealth of friendship, wealth of tradition, and wealth of spirit. They live in a very strong social community, and all around them are people who share their value system. They have no concept of poverty because everyone around them experiences lives so similar to their own. Their wealth is whatever the sea provides or what they can forage or hunt in the forests. The world is theirs even it is the small, small world of their village. They have no care about taxes, inflation, crime, or traffic. They are not bullied by social media posts. They don't need to upgrade their phones to the latest technology. Life and death are interwoven in ceremony. They are, by my estimate, quite rich.

Poverty is relative.
If people could simply take the time to acknowledge that there is a society all around them and that they have the capability to affect that society, they would find wealth that is more valuable than gold. Where we place our treasure is where we will place our hearts. Your treasure should be in the people you affect, not the material riches you possess.

Don't misunderstand. I am not against material wealth. I have obviously acquired it for myself. But I have done it in a way that has made me stronger and better. The hunt for money can easily rob you of your soul. So many will stab their friend in the back just to make a business deal. I have had so many business interests that I never had to stake my life on any single one. If something failed, I moved on to another. But I held on to the relationship because that is a currency that never loses value.

Chapter Ten

Hardening

The most beautiful people we have known are those who have known defeat, known suffering, known struggle, known loss, and have found their way out of the depths. These persons have an appreciation, a sensitivity, and an understanding of life that fills them with compassion, gentleness, and a deep loving concern. Beautiful people do not just happen."

~ Elisabeth Kübler-Ross

At this point in the discussion, you might be thinking back to some tough moments in your life and wondering how those awful moments might have been made better. The answer to this question is hardening.

Contrary to its name, hardening is not meant to suggest that you should become hardened or that your heart needs to be made of stone. Instead, hardening refers to building yourself up in the good times to prepare you for the bad times. Doing deep work, both inside and out, puts you in the best position to withstand the ups and downs.

Tough times are inevitable. None of us can escape them. As the old song goes, "Into each life, some rain must fall." Even though some people think they have bad luck or that unfortunate things happen to them more than others, statistically speaking, it isn't true. We all have loved ones who have died. We have all been hurt by a close friend. We have all misfortune with regard to our finances. What separates one person from another is how they navigate challenging times.

Some readers might be thinking that money is a factor. But even money cannot spare us from the difficulties of life. The rain falls on the rich and poor alike. Consider Steve Jobs, who, without argument, had enough money to hire the world's most outstanding doctors. But once his cancer spread, there was nothing he or anyone could do to change his outcome. The same is true of love. We may be surrounded by warm bodies, but simply having people around is not enough to buy love.

Marelisa Fabrega of the blog "Daring to Live Fully" writes about the difference between what money can buy and what it can't. The following are just a sample of what she lists:

Money can buy medicine, but it can't buy health.

Money can buy a house, but it can't buy a home.

Money can buy acquaintances but not friends.

Money can buy adulation but not respect.

Money can buy books, but it can't buy knowledge, wisdom, and experience.

Money can buy a life of leisure, but it can't buy purpose, passion, or meaning.

Money can buy watches, but it can't buy time.

***

The assumption that money is the answer to all of life's problems is a fallacy. It is difficult for people who don't have money to believe the truth in this statement because the problems they are dealing with, they believe, are based on their lack of funds. But many who have gone from poverty to wealth will tell you that money is no panacea.

Therefore, you must spend currency that doesn't jingle or fold. It is the kind of currency that can help you weather even the most turbulent storms of life.

My life was a roller coaster. In fact, it was a series of roller coasters all strung together into one terrifying ride. The highs were extremely high; the lows were often devastating. I felt like I was never going to reach the point where I could stop the ride and get off.

But, once I learned the concept of hardening, it became much easier to withstand. I developed an iron inner strength along with physical care that kept me strong when life threw punches my way.

I learned to find equilibrium at all times. While it's great to celebrate the exciting times of life and normal to feel down when adversity strikes, it is not healthy to be tossed around by fluctuations of life.

Take our current social media culture, for example. You might write a post that gets lots of praise. You immediately feel happy and excited. Then the first negative comment comes along. And, sometimes, it can be exceptionally negative, cruel, and hurtful. Suddenly, that feeling of pride in your post is dashed, and you lose a significant amount of that warm glow that was present just moments earlier. Now take it from the relatively low stakes world of social media to the high stakes realm of business or relationships. Perhaps you wrote a report which your colleagues loved. Then, when your boss read it, the negative feedback was devastating. Or imagine having a successful dating life until someone you especially enjoyed spending time with announced that they were no longer interested.

The power of hardening starts with learning not to let highs get too high and not to let lows get too low. Your grandparents called it "taking everything in stride." It's a physical reference to running a race and pacing yourself throughout the course of the race. Life is very much like a race. If you run ahead, you may run out of steam. If you hesitate, you may lag behind. Finding your pace and keeping that steady pace is the best strategy for longevity in the race of life.

The hardening process is used throughout the physical world to ensure the life of elements. Plants, for example, are often started as seeds indoors. They are placed in optimal conditions with near-perfect soil, water, and artificial sunlight. Timers ensure that the light is on part of the time and off for several hours of the day to allow plants the necessary darkness we covered earlier. One would think that seedlings grown in such a perfect environment would fare well as adult plants over their lifetimes. But these plants rarely survive when placed outside unless they are first hardened. They wither under the blistering sun and bow to the slightest wind without hardening.

Hardening plants involves removing them from their perfect environment and placing them in the real world for a short time. Each day, their exposure to the element is increased until they learn how to survive outside of the incubator.

The same process of hardening is applied to many other elements. Steel, for example, is forged in fire so it can be shaped. But then it must be cooled in oil so that it can be hardened. This harsh process is necessary for the steel to perform under extreme pressure.

Even systems must be hardened if they are going to survive. Banks and corporations, for example, must run simulations where they subject their institutions to stress to see how they will survive under different conditions. Wherever they fail, hardening of their operations must take place.

You are no different. While we would all wish to have a paradise where there is no pain, no sickness, no loss, and no death, the universe has a different plan. It will order and serve both good and bad times for you. If you are hardened, you can survive almost anything. But if you take the attitude that you will wait until something happens and deal with it, you may get blindsided and find it hard, if not impossible, to recover.

In the coming chapter, we will review several ways to harden yourself financially, spiritually, emotionally/mentally, and physically.

Struggles

My-mindguide.com

Chapter Eleven

Hardening Off

"For me, trees have always been the most penetrating preachers. I revere them when they live in tribes and families, in forests and groves. And even more I revere them when they stand alone. They are like lonely persons...

In their highest boughs the world rustles, their roots rest in infinity; but they do not lose themselves there, they struggle with all the force of their lives for one thing only: to fulfill themselves according to their own laws, to build up their own form, to represent themselves.

...Nothing is holier, nothing is more exemplary than a beautiful, strong tree. When a tree is cut down and reveals its naked death-wound to the sun, one can read its whole history in the luminous, inscribed disk of its trunk: in the rings of its years, its scars, all the struggle, all the suffering, the sickness, all the happiness and prosperity stand truly written, the narrow years and the luxurious years, the attacks withstood, the storms endured. And every young farmboy knows that the hardest and noblest wood has the narrowest rings, that high on the mountains and in continuing danger the most indestructible, the strongest, the ideal trees grow.

~ Herman Hesse, Bäume: Betrachtungen und Gedichte

Hardening has favorable applications in many areas of your life. In this chapter, we will explore some practical ways to harden yourself so that you are well-equipped to handle whatever comes your way.

Financial Hardening

This same strategy can be applied to your finances. Are you one of those people who live paycheck to paycheck? Or have you received your income tax return or a surprise bonus check only to find that it is all gone in a week or two? Your mindset about money will determine whether you are a marathoner or a sprinter.

You may have heard that slow and steady wins the race when it comes to money. Slow may not be necessary. But steady is definitely a powerful pace to take with money. Don't allow yourself to be fooled about how money actually works. There was a time when I was thirty when I broke through a million dollars in net worth. I was overjoyed. I had worked hard for a long time to get there. However, my response to being a millionaire wasn't to go out and buy a Porsche or plan a holiday in paradise. I knew that the good times I was experiencing were bound to be followed by bad times, just like winter follows fall. I decided that I would save money so that I would not find myself in despair when things took a downturn. I set some money aside for luxuries and kept working. I kept the same pace on the next major upturn, setting aside a bit more in savings and reserving some for luxuries.

As a result, I never reached a point where I was in despair. The stock market went up and down. The value of real estate fluctuated all over the spectrum. Economies changed year after year. But my fortune was safe because I kept my steady pace and was never in a state of despair. That is the essence of hardening yourself financially.

Saving is one of the best ways to harden your finances. Various financial gurus have different strategies for how to save, how much you should save, and where you should place your savings. That is not my role here. My job is to convince you to harden yourself against inevitable economic difficulties. How do I know for sure economic strife is coming? Because economic strife always comes. It's just a matter of time. World economics correct themselves after times of great prosperity. To think otherwise is to live in a fantasy. So, think about where you want to be when the markets crash, wars are raging, or corporate or political changes upset your finances.

My second strategy was learning to invest. I emphasize learning because investing is a school from which you never graduate. With every lesson comes a dozen more you must learn. And, as soon as you know something for sure, something changes and places you right back in the classroom to learn again. For example, even seasoned investors who have been in the game for decades have had to learn the ins and outs of cryptocurrency. And our education isn't over as world governments decide if and how they will regulate it and tax it. Investing in gold, crypto, real estate, or other markets can be engaging and lucrative. But it can also be a wipeout where you lose all your cash if you approach it as an expert rather than a student.

Mental Hardening

One of my favorite topics to cover is mental hardening. It is something almost anyone can do regardless of their level of wealth, education, or social status. Most people in the world have smartphones. The statistics show that, even in undeveloped countries, cell phones can be found. A Statista survey calculated global cell phone use at 83.6 percent. Even in countries where cell phone use is limited, access to new knowledge is still strong as long as it is not connected to political interests. In other words, if you could buy this book, you can learn.

This is one of the reasons I chose to become addicted to discipline rather than alcohol or drugs. Knowledge is power. And it was my goal always to maintain a sharp mind. While I don't condemn substances, I acknowledge their effect on the ability to think. I live from my mind. So do you. Everything about you starts with the mind. Every movement of the body. Every decision you make. Where you go, what you do, and the attitudes that drive you all start in the mind. If your mind is sharp and alert, nothing is impossible for you.

So how do we go about hardening the mind?
First, fight your battles in secret. Many people want to broadcast their struggles to the world. They are searching for sympathy more than answers. They want people to identify with them and commiserate about their problems. Fighting secret battles builds inner strength. Times of quiet introspection can do far more than messages of support from our Facebook friends.

Enlist trusted mentors. Just because you are dealing with your tough times in secret doesn't mean that you have to deal with them alone. Determine carefully who you can trust to share your deepest secrets. Most people can't handle them and sometimes fail to keep confidences. One or two trusted advisers will help elevate the conversation about what you are dealing with so that it becomes more than just bellyaching. Instead, it becomes a strategy session to talk over solutions and best practices.

Stay objective in tough times. Remember our discussion of being steady regardless of the good or bad circumstances surrounding you? Doing so can help to develop a strong mind. Continuing to show up and do the things you are responsible for builds mental toughness.

Have your own opinion. A study was conducted where a group of ten participants were shown three lines — line A, line B, and line C. One of the three lines, line B, was clearly longer than the other two. However, most people in the room chose either line A or line C. Why? Nine people in the room were told not to select line B. Only one person was being studied. The rest of the group were there as actors, allowing researchers to see if that person could maintain their opinion in the face of opposing perspectives and ideas.

While it is always wise to consider the opinions of others, it is not wise to alter your perspective simply to match the perspective of others. Developing mental toughness means standing by your carefully reasoned view even in the face of opposition.

Mental toughness also involves the ability to change when needed. Keeping the prior paragraph in mind, you develop mental toughness when presented with facts that demand a change in direction or opinion. Remaining dogged in your opinion when it has become clear that you are wrong weakens your mental capacity as well as your reputation. Once all the facts are in, weigh them as if you have no stake in the outcome. Then choose the course of action that is best. That may mean making a change in your prior stance.

Emotional Hardening

We are a thinking species. But we are also a feeling species. Our emotions are not our enemies. They are designed to help us understand the world around us and keep ourselves safe. Our emotions alert us to how our environment impacts us and, hopefully, warn us when there is danger. They are also attracting us to things that are helpful and good for us.

However, when emotions grow out of our control, they are no longer helping us. Instead, they blow every stimulus far out of proportion and make us incapable of choosing carefully and wisely. You have seen people who appear to be behaving purely based on emotion (perhaps that person was you). They are hard to communicate with. They make rash decisions. Their mistakes compound over time until they have created such a tangled web that it is hard to unravel and put the pieces of their lives back in their proper places. Living as hyperemotional people makes them vulnerable to attack from even the slightest threat. They live in a constant state of fear, anxiety, and mistrust.

Emotions that grow out of control keep us in a survival state and prevent us from expressing our true selves. As you experience the emotions connected to the true self, you can use them as a tool. Your thinking and behavior will remain congruent with the higher vibration emotions like love, compassion, forgiveness, and gratitude. As you break away from the survival forms of yourself, you will come to find that your thoughts can work in alignment with your emotions as you deal with day-to-day issues, problems, and pain, as well as those crisis moments that arise.

Advances in technology have brought the need for hardening in the cyber world. Cyber-attacks can destroy companies and governments and compromise millions of consumers' personal information. So, companies have had to learn to harden their presence on the internet to ensure they can survive an attack. It seems every sector of our world has to think about hardening.

It is this type of systems hardening model that we will adopt as we look at how we can address weak areas in our lives. Systems hardening is a four-step process: audit, identify, close, and control.

In the audit phase, we will look at our current state as it is, not as we wish it was or as we thought it was before we examined it closely. The audit is meant to be completely dispassionate. It is merely asking yourself:

- Where am I?
- How am I handling the issues in my life, both good and bad?
- Am I generous and kind when I should be?
- Am I firm and non-negotiable when I should be?
- Am I caring for myself thoughtfully?
- Am I caring for others in a healthy way that helps them without compromising my value system?
- Am I financially alert to all of the issues surrounding my spending, access to credit, saving, and investing?

- Are my relationships healthy and mutually beneficial?
- Do I feel mentally strong, or could I benefit from some help?
- Is my body a reflection of the consistent care I provide myself inside and out?
- Do my actions reflect the spiritual disciplines I claim to embrace, or are there areas of contradiction?

In the "identify" phase, we simply pick out the areas that appear weak and unprotected. We know that acknowledgment is the first step to growth. You cannot fix what you won't admit is broken. In this phase, each area is simply accounted for so that the next step can occur.

The "close" phase involves taking each identified area and developing a detailed and specific strategy for addressing how the area can be hardened. This is not a wish list of esoteric hopes and goals. Instead, specific action steps need to be outlined and committed to.

The "control" phase brings these processes together because you can only manage what you can measure. In the control phase, you perform self-evaluation to determine whether or not the action steps you have implemented are achieving their desired goals. If they are, you can decide if you want to maintain them or accelerate them. If they are not, however, it is time to go back to the identification phase. Did you isolate the proper concern? If you are certain you did, then something was wrong within the control phase.

One caveat: making changes in your life takes time. Imagine a large ocean liner when it has to make a turn. It takes very small corrections over many hours to get the ship moving in a different direction. Expecting to see significant improvement immediately will skew your evaluation. Consider tackling one area at a time and making a few minor changes.

For example, if your finances are out of whack, it would be a mistake to try to change everything. Instead, you might start with taking your credit cards out of your wallet, only spending cash, and setting aside a small amount of money for savings each week. Big changes are tough. Remember, "yard by yard is hard, but inch by inch is a cinch!"

Chapter Twelve

Sickness: Lessons of Life and Love

"The spirit is one of the most neglected parts of man by doctors and scientists around the world. Yet, it is as vital to our health as the heart and mind. It's time for science to examine the many facets of the soul. The condition of our soul is usually the source of many sicknesses."

~ *Suzy Kassem*, Rise Up and Salute the Sun:
The Writings of Suzy Kassem

In 2019, the first cases of COVID-19 were being reported in places around the world. Then, in 2020, western nations began to confess that their citizens had been infected and that, in short order, it would spread around the world without restraint. In response to the crisis, world governments asked their citizens to shelter in place. These lockdowns lasted for nearly two years, with many governments making them mandatory and demanding that people show vaccine passports to visit entertainment venues or eat in restaurants.

The pandemic changed life for people in almost every place it touched. Some of the changes were good. People learned more about how viruses spread and, hopefully, learned the benefit of good hygiene habits like washing their hands frequently and covering their coughs and sneezes. But there were some unintended consequences.

As the pandemic spread, many people lost their jobs. Some claimed they went to work one day and had been laid off or terminated by the next. It was a sad state of affairs. Hunger and poverty spread as fast as the coronavirus, and lines for free food grew.

But in 2021, vaccines were created and made available. Most countries offered them free of charge to the recipient. The spread seemed to slow. And, despite variants like Delta and Omicron, many countries partially or wholly re-opened. Still, many stores, schools, government offices, and other businesses remained closed. Why?

A visit to any local store at the end of 2021 or the start of 2022 revealed the symptoms of a growing illness in society. Help Wanted signs posted on the windows, the marquee, and in strategic places throughout the store signaled the hiring crisis facing employers in the U.S. and other countries worldwide. Workers in the U.S., for example, had gotten fat from government stimulus checks that supported them during the pandemic. Unemployment benefits were extended to unprecedented lengths, and government bonus money in the many thousands of dollars had killed the working spirit of many American citizens.

At the same time, internet usage and posts on social media were higher than ever. And a common recurring theme was a sense of despair among the world's youth over the crisis.

Generations X and Y appear spoiled and unable to maintain their motivation at the slightest provocation. Though much of the youth during the coronavirus pandemic had unlimited internet access, smartphones, and video games, many of them spent hours posting their sad videos about how the world was not making sense to them anymore. They saw this as the end of the world. They were unable to handle sudden changes even though they were least likely to contract the virus, have symptoms, be hospitalized, or die by all accounts of medical professionals.

Contrast this to the Greatest Generation who experienced poverty, war, hunger, and struggle, but emerged to lay the foundation for the greatest era in human history. They are marked by distinct qualities, as detailed by the man who coined the term, Tom Brokaw, in his book, *The Greatest Generation*. He writes that the Greatest Generation:

- Handled change well
  In the modern world, when the slightest bit of traffic or the mildest disappointment can send people flying into a rage, the Greatest Generation were people who had to constantly adapt to a rapidly changing world. Europe was enduring a shakeup, and the U.S. was finding its footing as a world leader. World War II broke out and changed daily life for two years and even through the following decade. This generation was marked by surviving tough times. They lived through the Great Depression and developed incredible coping skills

- Were not afraid of hard work
  Having lived through the Great Depression, this generation might have worked all day long just to earn five cents. They

learned the value of working hard since nearly everyone they knew was out of work. Only by working harder than the worker next to you could you be assured work the next day.

- Tended toward thriftiness
This was a generation that never wasted a thing. They threw nothing away. The wastefulness of the modern era where a broken item is trashed and replaced would shock members of the Great Depression era. They knew how to repair watches, rebuild broken furniture, and cook in a variety of environments. Food was never tossed out. It was often rationed but always eaten. Soup and bread lines to feed the unemployed, hungry, and homeless were long. So, wasting food was never an option.

- Believed in sacrifice
Many of the men enlisted in the military and served on the battlefield. But the women also played their roles. Few had the honor of service. But those who remained behind took up jobs in the factories to fill positions vacated by men. Others sewed uniforms. Some served as nurses. And others gathered metals to be used in the war effort.

Gen X and Y could learn a lot from this generation about surviving, adapting, and making do with little.

Struggles

My-mindguide.com

Chapter Thirteen

Failures and Fears

What hurts you blesses you. Darkness is your candle.
~ Rumi

OOO

The short answer to the question, "Who am I?" is this: You are who you say you are. Or, better stated, you are who you believe you are. If you believe that you are a product of the negative events that have happened in your life, you will act out of that belief. If you bow to your failures and fears, you will be forever defined by them.

We have explored some things that hold people back, the dark places of our lives where it becomes difficult to imagine a future much different from the present. We discussed the truth that, when you face obstacles, what matters is not the problem or the adversities you face, but your attitude about them and your approach in dealing with them. Obstacles can set ablaze your new passion or ambition. They form the path you must follow to become the person you are meant to be. There is no going around it. First, there is an obstacle which is your test. As you face it and overcome it, it becomes your testimony and triumph.

Thrill-seekers and nature lovers alike are always looking for new adventures and places that few people on Earth get to see. One of those places is Pulpit Rock in Norway, also called Preikstolen. It is not a terribly high climb, just 604 meters. Just getting to the top is one of the most stunning and picturesque journeys you can take. Your hike starts at the bottom of the massive rock. The range is dotted with magnificent green as trees push their way up out of the hardened granite landscape and rise to greet the sun and be nourished by the cool and refreshing rains. The range runs along the edge of a clear crystal water fjord that goes on for miles in the distance. It is the kind of splendid beauty created by a partnership between God and time almost 10,000 years in the making and existing since the Ice Age.

However, in the midst of this beauty and wonder is a terrifying and fatal threat: falling off the edge. You see, when you reach the summit of the rock, the nearly flat top of the rock, nothing is standing between you, and a 600-meter fall to your likely death. The custodians of the attraction elected not to spoil the beauty of the view with ropes, gates, glass walls, or any other barriers. You climb at your own risk. When you reach the top, you can stop and look out over the fjord. Or you can walk all the way to the edge until your toes tingle from the danger of one more step forward.

In 2013, reports on the local and global news were aired that a man visiting Pulpit Rock from Spain stepped too close to the edge, got dizzy, lost his balance, and fell off the side, plunging to his death on the crags below. Debate erupted from those in Norway and other places about the danger of the Rock, with some even suggesting that the popular tourist attraction that draws 300,000 visitors per year should be closed. On one side of the debate were those who love the hike and endure the challenging two- to three-hour walk to reach the top so that they can breathe in the breathtakingly expansive view. These Pulpit Rock enthusiasts fought to keep it open. Their argument was sound, suggesting that the introduction of a fence would obscure the near-heavenly vision of the fjord. They even argued that the beauty of the steep drop-off as it plunged its way down into fjord was as delightful as the water. Others advised that the attraction created too extreme of a risk. Public safety at the site had to be considered above all else. The death of this man, they felt, was a cautionary tale. Norwegian government leaders suggested a compromise, requesting that a very small safety fence be placed to act as a barrier. It would help, they said, to caution a careless person from stepping out too far and accidentally falling off the sharp edge.

Many tourists pointed out a keen and persuasive element about Pulpit Rock that, perhaps, those concerned with safety had not calculated in their deliberations: the many thousands of people had made the journey over the years since the attraction opened expressly for the danger. They loved challenging themselves by making it up the mountain and coming close to the edge. They found something inside themselves, courage, daring, who knows, that was expressed in coming to the Rock. They faced and conquered fear through this unique experience. Any barrier would lessen the challenge and, thereby, cheapen the reward.

Surprisingly, it wasn't just adults making the trek up Pulpit Rock. A large percentage of the hikers reaching the summit were children. With their affinity for adventure and aversion to fear, children happily strolled out onto the cliff and sat right on the edge, courting the jaws of death while happily swinging their tiny legs back and forth. They seemed to be wholly unfazed by the risk of being torn to bits should they wobble off the edge. And yet, not one of them had ever been harmed. After listening to both sides, the officials of Pulpit Rock reopened the attraction without making any changes. This time, the argument that facing fear is better than being shielded from it won.

There is another lesson to be learned from Pulpit Rock. That lesson comes to us from the climbers who reach the summit and see a fairly easy, straight, flat rock leading to the edge where the views are best. It is what they climbed to see. But once they see the striking granite plateau that juts out toward the terrifying drop-off and sinks down into the lovely Lyse Fjord, they are unable to take even a single step forward. They stop, frozen in place. There they stand, armed with an expensive camera and a desire to walk out to see the views, but they cannot take a single step. After spending the time and money to come to Norway and making it all the way up the hill, they pause before reaching their iconic prize. They have reached the edge of one of the most awe-inspiring places on earth, but they know that their journey is not over. Their goal was never just to reach the top of the precipice. The goal was to walk across the plateau to the edge and press their toes against the brink.

They stand there as hundreds of people pass them from the bottom, anxious to run over to the edge, and hundreds pass them from the top, intoxicated by what they had just experienced. But for those locked and frozen, it is a failure. Their vision was not focused on the fjord. It is, instead, focused on the image of themselves tumbling hundreds of feet over the edge as their bodies break apart on the sharp crags while friends and visitors look on in horror.

These people have something to learn about themselves. They must come face-to-face with more than their fear. They must confront their own imaginations and the visions they bow to. They must deal with their goals and their commitment to them. To come so close to success and fall paralyzed, they must have some powerful paradigms playing out in their minds. This is a darkness of the soul, a place that haunts them. Little did they know that the same fear that lay in the darkness of the minds was astride the courage they needed to take the first step. After the first step, they would have taken the second. Inch by inch, they would have made it. And with each step, more of that glorious view they sought would have become visible. They would have achieved immortality, if only for a moment.

We use the word "living" to describe the state of breathing, being conscious, etc. But living has a deeper connotation that can only be captured in moments of extreme beauty, deep love, connection with the earth, or stepping onto the other side of fear. Moving past fear reveals a world you suspected was there but did not previously have evidence to prove its existence. How do we ensure we are living? Do we hide away from struggle, risk, and fear, remaining content merely in knowing that we are inhaling and exhaling? Or, do we remove the insulation that keeps us safe from danger so that we can uncover who we might really be? I opt for the latter.

> *God put the best things in life on the other side of fear.*
> *~Will Smith*

***

Where do you see yourself on the metaphorical hike up to Pulpit Rock? Are you still standing at the bottom of the mountain looking up, too unwilling to commit the demanding and challenging climb? Or are you on your way, taking step after step on the journey up the mountain? Are you standing beside the poor souls who managed to reach the top but were too afraid to take the few steps to the edge? Or are you all in with life, willing to go to the other side of your fear to experience the best life has to offer you?

I know what it means to have fear and death stare me down and refuse to back down. Death was possible at many stages of my young life. But I decided not to back down to it. I wish for you that same determination and courage. The payoff is that you get to write the destiny you will live. I encourage you to step to the edge, see what life has to offer you, and catch the amazing view.

How can you tell when you are coming close to the brink of greatness? There are many ways. But, fear is one way to know that something important is about to happen in your life. In that way, fear is your friend because it warns you that something special is taking place. The height of your fear might also be the height of your opportunity. Fear gets a bad rap, and we do everything we can to avoid it. Instead, we should seek to control it and face it. Don't struggle against your fear. Ask yourself what the fear is trying to tell you. Don't run from it.

Meditation and mindfulness can be powerful tools to help you control your fear. Through meditation, you learn to harness the power of the mind. Meditation expert Jack Kornfield writes:

Although most of us have been deeply conditioned by fear, for the most part we have avoided directly exploring its nature. Because we are not aware of its workings, it is often an unconscious driving force in our lives. When fear arises, whether it's fear of pain, fear of certain emotions, or fear of death, the meditation practice of mindful loving awareness invites us to explore and understand fear itself. What does it feel like? What are the sensations in the body? Where are they located? Are there images or pictures in the mind? We can look closely to see the constellation of experiences we call fear, to understand its true nature. When we do so, we see that fear is also a passing conditioned experience, and then it becomes much more workable.

Start simply. When fear arises, name it softly and experience what it does to the breath, to the body, how it affects the heart. Notice how long it lasts. Be aware of the images. Notice the sensations and ideas that accompany it, the scary stories it tells. Fear is often an anticipation of the future, an imagination, often unfounded. As Mark Twain remarked, "My life has been filled with terrible misfortunes—most of which never happened."

Of course, when we work with the fearful mind, we will initially become afraid. However, at some point, if we open our eyes and our heart to the fearful mind and gently name it, "fear, fear, fear," experiencing its energy as it moves through us, the whole sense of fear will shift and eventually become recognition: "Oh, fear, here you are again. I know you. How interesting that you've come." Make friends with your fear.

***

Fear can be a powerful helper, enabling us to recognize big and important moments in our lives. Anytime we are faced with fear, we have various choices for what our response will be. Some fears tell us that the best course of action is to run from impending danger. Other situations might call for running toward danger, like rescuing someone who is drowning.

Fear is an equal opportunity emotion and shows up in both good situations and bad. It can be present as you move toward success as well as failure. We might feel a tinge of fear as we stand before the minister on our wedding day, and we might feel fear if we land in court and have to face a judge. Just know that, whatever the situation, you are equipped to handle it. In fact, it might be helpful to declare those words as a mantra. "I can handle this." Speaking those words again and again helps you establish your resolve. No one gets to escape the emotion of fear. But all of us can learn to manage and handle it better.

There is so much freedom in finding your footing when it comes to fear. Sometimes fear is just exhilaration that comes when you feel a wave of excitement you have never felt before. Exhilaration is a powerful concept with many levels to unpack. But let's just identify one. Its first documented appearance in literature was when it described "the making of a happy heart." This is a lovely word derived from the same root word as hilarious or hilarity. It is the kind of joy and a special type of laughter that doesn't come from hearing something comical, but that emerges when one is doing something or experiencing something that makes the heart truly glad. It cannot be contained by or expressed with a smile. It generates a type of exuberance that arises from the soul and is infectious.

This is the kind of joy experienced by Alex Honnold, whose claim to fame is a type of rock climbing called free solo, where the climber scales the rock alone with no safety equipment. It is perilous and has been responsible for many deaths. However, it brings Alex, and others who practice it, that kind of exhilaration we explored. His life is chronicled in a documentary exploring his climb up El Capitan in Yosemite National Park in the U.S. One of the most poignant moments in the film occurs when Alex reaches the top of El Capitan. Though he is a quiet and somber young man who rarely cracks so much as a smile, you can see that he is overcome with emotion when he steps his foot on the top of the rock. He shakes with excitement and laughs out loud. Exhilaration. He then looks back over the rock he just scaled with nothing but mere nerve, steel will, and a bit of chalk to keep his hands dry.

One might wonder why someone would put their life in danger in such a way. It seems reckless. After all, there is no real purpose in climbing the rock this way other than to say you did. But that is what Alex believes he was created to do. Without it, his life would be incomplete. The fear is not enough to stop him. The risk of death is not enough to stop him. The pleas of his family are not enough to stop him. He must climb rocks. So, he does.

Nothing can compare to doing what you say you will do. Even if there is danger or risk, you feel inexplicably drawn to it. The night before Alex's climbs, he sleeps in a trailer at the foot of the rock. In the darkness, he reconciles his fear and nervousness. He counts the cost of his decision, reminds himself of his training, and then drifts off to sleep.

A motivational speaker once cautioned his audience to limit the amount of time they watched tv. He explained that people who appear on television were already living their dream. Viewers are numbly watching them do what they were born to do. The speaker suggested that each audience member needed to get busy living their own dreams rather than watching others live theirs.

Modern humans consume a staggering amount of television, YouTube, and social media. Most people touch their cell phones over a hundred times per day. An overwhelming majority of them sleep with their phones and even take them along to the bathroom. It is as if we have become a world of people entranced, spellbound by others enjoying their lives while we complain about ours. I don't mean to suggest that there is no value in television. Much of it is educational and informative. But much of it is in mindless attempts at holding an audience's attention. The bar continues to drop lower and lower.

What's worse is that television viewing among children is worse than with adults. The Nielsen Company reported that kids watch as many as six hours of television each day. It is no coincidence that this generation of youth is sicker, fatter, and more depressed than their predecessors.

There are tons of activities kids could engage in that would give them the same kind of exhilaration Alex Honnold has found. They could spend their days searching for the one big thing that motivates and inspires them.

Chapter Fourteen

Awareness

We have learned that the subconscious mind is many times more powerful than the conscious mind. It plays back all of our doubts and fears. It rehearses our mistakes like they are a tape playing on a loop. By exercising awareness, we can listen to the recording and make a different choice about what we will believe. When we are aware, we observe our thoughts, actions, beliefs, emotions, and mistakes. We get to check our behavior and mindset, knowing we will need to have them in line to move forward. Awareness is the process of moving from the passenger seat to the driver's seat and taking control of the steering wheel of our lives.

When we are aware, we are fully present in each daily activity as it is happening. We remain in the now — in the moment. When we are not aware and fully present, the images of the past override our thoughts. Depression can be sparked by consistently thinking about the past or having anxiety, worry, and fear of the future. The sweet spot is in the present – here and now while we work toward future goals.

All life forms display survival behaviors. All animals do as well as individual cells within the body. When a cell is in a petri dish and a toxin is introduced, over time, the cells will move to the other side to get as far away from the threat as they can. Conversely, if some sort of food source is placed in the dish that the cells can use, they will move toward it over time. We are a collection of 50 trillion cells. And we cannot move both toward and away at the same time. We are either in survival mode of self-preservation, or we are in creation mode.

Through awareness, we address whether our thoughts or behaviors are self-protective or creative. By choosing to be creative more than protective, we can start to change the program.

The ability to observe or own thoughts and behavior is known as metacognition. It is important to remember we are not our thoughts. Through awareness, we can watch a negative thought and select something different for ourselves. We can choose something better, greater, and more aligned with our purpose and passion.

Until we make peace with exactly how things are, we cannot start working toward the future and empower ourselves to be in the driver's seat. We drive ourselves into a survival state if we refuse to accept what is.

Accepting responsibility for the here and now is where our real power begins. Understand that you possess the ability to shape your present and future. The faster you find acceptance, the quicker you return to the present moment. When you are focused on and lamenting over the past, you are not in the present. You are trapped in the past and blocked from the beautiful present.

The brain is always looking for value. If you train your brain to find value in drama, heartache, and sadness, it will always search for that. But, when you expand your world to find other places of meaning, you teach your mind to find value in more positive places.

One of the fastest ways to change your state of being from depression, anger, anxiety, and addiction is to take action. The action comes first. Then comes the relief, followed by exhilaration. You will find that the other areas of your life begin to line up with your new expression. When you move, the universe moves to meet you. And you don't have to make massive shifts. Even the slightest bend of the rudder can, eventually, turn a big ship.

Sitting in a state of frustration or blame, attempting to use the same thinking and feelings that created the problem can only produce more of the same. You can only amplify the problem. Something as simple as standing, putting on your shoes, and going for a 10-minute walk around the block breaks the redundant cycle of negative thoughts producing negative feelings that, then, produce more negative thoughts. Deepening your awareness through meditation or hypnotherapy can take you to the next level.

Far too many people are trying to think their way out of the issues they find themselves in without realizing that their thinking (mindset) has played the most prominent role in creating the very problems they are experiencing. It's the same with allowing our survival emotions to dictate our mindset. If we feel anger, guilt, shame, frustration, or blame and don't change our state of being by taking action and breaking our environment, we can only drive thoughts equal to those survival emotions. When you feel rage, you think rageful thoughts. When you feel the chemistry in your body of guilt and shame, it is a signal of what the mind is focused on.

Be aware of where you are and what you are thinking. The key is – if it is to be, it is up to me. So, take an action that sandblasts you out of where you are to a more enlightened place. Some actions you can take are:

- Walking
- Going to the Gym
- Taking a swim
- Meditation
- Writing out your goals
- Calling a friend (never use a friend as a sounding board to reaffirm your state of being)

Ask yourself what you want more: the pain of your past or the limitless potential that lies in your future. Remember every decision we make either recreates the events of our past so that we stay in a predictable comfort zone, or chooses our future while stepping out into the unknown.

Heightened awareness is a journey… a practice. Be gentle with yourself as you grow. Have the courage to offer yourself compassion. Congratulate yourself for each step forward. But don't get stuck in self-praise. Keep moving.

Anthony K. Tjan of Harvard Business writes about how awareness impacts your business as well as your home:

Meditate. Yes, meditate. As most people know by now, meditation is the practice of improving your moment-by-moment awareness. Most forms of meditation begin with focusing on and appreciating the simplicity of inhaling and exhaling. But these don't need to be formal or ritualistic — greater clarity can also come from regular moments of pause and reflection. Speaking personally, I try to gain greater awareness by simply finding a few seconds to focus on my breathing, often before sleep, and sometimes with one of the many apps available to help. During these meditations, I also ask myself a set of questions, among them:

- *What am I trying to achieve?*
- *What am I doing that is working?*
- *What am I doing that is slowing me down?*
- *What can I do to change?*

Write down your key plans and priorities. One of the best ways to increase self-awareness is to write down what you want to do and track your progress. Warren Buffet, for one, is known for carefully articulating the reasons he's making an investment at the time he makes it. His journal entries serve as a historical record that helps him assess whether or not future outcomes can be attributable to sound judgment or just plain luck.

Benjamin Franklin kept a "balance sheet" of both the assets and liabilities of his personal traits. By diarizing any new strengths he believed he could learn from someone else, and marking down any self-perceived weaknesses, he could better assess whether the "net worth" of his character was growing over time.

Lack of awareness of your true self and failure to accept who you are today can keep you bound and stuck. You will always strive to meet a standard that is impossible to achieve. Yes, you are transforming. But the foundation of your transformation must be the acceptance of who you are today—and it must come from a place of love and forgiveness. The emotions connected to the true self where our love, passion, courage, creativity, and sense of purpose lie are the emotions we should explore. Any emotion that takes you away from the place of love, acceptance, and faith is an emotion to move away from.

The primary emotions connected to the true self that you should be seeking are:

Love (ultimate connection to and affection for others)

Compassion (the ability to feel the pain of others and respond appropriately)

Assertiveness (speaking your truth, defending the defenseless, being congruent with your values, standing and speaking for truth, establishing boundaries)

Gratitude (ultimate state of acknowledging the gift of life you've received. Through it, we find responsibility and a sense of purpose)

Exhilaration (the feeling of pure joy that comes from the realization of a worthy goal that produces a happy heart)

These positive expressions of life make our existence rich and full. The negative emotions (greed, hatred, anger, etc.) are the negative expressions of life. By remaining in a state of awareness, you can evaluate what triggers move you away from the positive and into the negative. Once you are aware, you can choose again more mindfully.

Find your Courage

*It takes more courage to examine the dark corners of your own soul
than it does for a soldier to fight on a battlefield.*
~ William Butler Yeats

It takes far more courage to be emotionally vulnerable than it does to react and move into rage and violence. Yet, most people respond to life's events by acting, especially when they feel helpless and out of control. Finding courage starts with having the bravery to be authentically you. Knowing yourself is your most outstanding achievement because it is from that knowledge that you are able to evolve. Your purest expression of self is the foundation of everything of purpose you will do in the world.

Courage to be you means being connected with each part of yourself: your emotions, your purpose, and your failures. All of them matter.

Courage with Emotions
Your emotions are an essential element of the true self. They encompass your sadness, joy, and concerns. The word "emotion" originates from the Old French word that means

"energy in motion" or "to get movement from." Your emotions should not rule your behaviors, but serve as a guide to help you understand how you think or feel about a situation.

At times, your emotions may try to take a power position and urge you to do or not do something. Don't let your feelings vote. Remain in an empowered, assertive position that considers all of the data available to you. Your emotions are only part of that equation.

Courage to face your emotions means learning to accept that you feel a certain way and then deciding what your response to those feelings will be. Sometimes you will determine what you feel is appropriate to the situation, and you should explore those emotions. At other times, you may decide that your feelings have fallen into a spiral and, if you obey them, you may make an error in judgment.

All in all, feelings are never bad or wrong. They are just present to give us more information. When feelings are combined with objectivity and reason, we can make decisions more wisely.

All of the emotions connected to our true selves keep us in a position of self-empowerment where we are dynamic, free-thinking, and expressive. All of the emotions controlled or prompted by external forces that cause us to spiral, move us from a position of power to a victim's mindset, where we believe the world is happening to us and we have no power to change the event.

While there are some rare situations when there is truly nothing we can do, the vast majority of life's problems demand a response from us. We are able to shape and guide the course of our lives rather than being tossed this way and that way by events we deem outside of our control. Very little is outside of our control.

The true self is expressed when we connect with the courage required to be vulnerable and feel genuine emotions. For many of us, it is sorrow, sadness, and grief that we block, which is resistance to what is happening in our lives at the moment. This is the definition of suffering. Rather than face our emotions head-on and evaluate what we might do in any given situation to change it for the better, we give up and express our helplessness as rage, depression, addiction, blame, self-hate, etc. These are outward manifestations of inner confusion when emotions are swirling around with no place to land.

The journey of transformation to a strong, confident, thinking, and reasoning self is not a quick fix, overnight, pop-a-pill response that causes your troubles to vanish away suddenly. You are creating the masterpiece that is your true self. It cannot be rushed. It cannot be found on an app. There is no one place to go to get strong in your emotions. There is no shortcut to growing emotionally. There is only focused action repeated over time.

Courage to Find Purpose

Finding courage requires consistent action in the direction of your journey over time. It requires you to always be in a state of asking. Asking yourself meaningful questions is one of the greatest exercises you can do because it reveals the true self and confirms that you have many of the answers you seek.

Thousands of books have been written on this concept, and thousands more will follow. Why do so many people write and read about purpose? I believe that it is because purpose is our greatest desire. Everything we want and need is connected to our reason for being. Purpose is the first of the great four questions of life:

- What is my purpose?
- How do I know right from wrong?
- Where did I come from?
- What happens when I die?

It is fair to say that the majority of people have had to grapple with these questions. We are all trying to understand the meaning of life. "What is my purpose?" "What is my role in this world?" "What is my role in each situation specifically?" "What is my true potential?"

Then, go out into the world and act accordingly. To step into your power and find the courage to be emotionally congruent will free you from the past and empower the now.

This is why you must dig deep, get clear on what you really want in this life, and connect with your resolve. Your purpose is akin to the description of pirate behavior whenever they seized a great treasure — they buried it. The search for purpose and meaning outside of yourself will leave you always searching. It is a fool's errand. Meaning and resolve will never come if you look outward for purpose.

Instead, summon the courage to look within to discover purpose. This may be terrifying at first, especially if you have believed negative paradigms about yourself. Years of self-deprecation and failure to live up to your true potential may leave you believing there is little value to searching within. But just as the fictional pirates buried their treasure in the dirt, your purpose may be buried under a cover of bad ideas, failures, wrong belief systems, and other muck. You will have to shovel past all that to strike gold.

Courage to Face Failure

There are both past failures and fear of future failures. Each has its own dragons to face. First, let's look at past failures.

You probably already know that you can't move into a new destiny holding onto the shame or pain of the past. Past failures can sometimes function as anchors. Just as a large anchor is designed to keep a ship in place, your own past failures can hold you in the place where you made the error.

So, the progression looks like this: you want to start a business, get excited about the prospects, and set a plan in motion. Then you get an error message. The past objects to your desire to move forward by reminding you of the business you started that did not succeed, the friend who lost everything in a business bid, or the mountain of paperwork and red tape you have to complete.

Or, perhaps you meet an intriguing romantic prospect. You agree to a first date. Things are looking great. But then the past sends an error message. You remember your last messy breakup or a long, rough divorce. You think about all your flaws or even the potential flaws the other person might have.

In these times, when you receive these error messages, your character gets tested. Tests of character are good when you respond to them appropriately. A test is designed to show you where you are in a particular subject area. A character test reveals chinks in your armor. If you respond by shrinking away and declaring that all is lost, you fail the test. However, if you respond by working on the places in your character that need repair, you win.

You should never succumb to the negative thought patterns that automatically come up. You can hear your mind screaming them at you:

- *I am not enough.*
- *I am broken.*
- *I don't have enough knowledge.*
- *I am a bad person.*
- *I did a bad thing.*
- *I don't have what it takes.*

These are just a sampling of the error messages you will receive when you try to move forward. They are the anchors that keep your proverbial ship from sailing. You worry that you will make the same or a similar mistake. And you indeed may if you have not taken the critical step of looking at the past error and dissecting it. If this is the case, it will always be there to threaten you and keep you from seizing what lies ahead. So many people who are doing whatever they can to avoid experiencing the pain of the past find that they remain imprisoned by an event that took place years, if not decades, earlier.

Instead, they might say this of that failed business:
- *I learned so much from that failure. (Then, list the lessons learned.)*
- *That failed business represents a host of mistakes I will never make again.*
- *I've been through the paperwork, so it will be at least a bit easier this time.*
- *I will not approach this business with the fear of the past. This is a new start.*

And, they might say or ask this of that failed relationship:
- *What did I do to contribute to the breakdown of the relationship?*
- *Did I choose poorly or perform poorly?*
- *If I chose poorly, what character deficiencies was I willing to overlook to have that relationship?*
- *What baggage did I bring to the relationship that weighed it down?*
- *Did I enter the relationship with the wrong expectations?*

This is the kind of introspection that builds us up rather than tears us down.

When you fail, you don't get to beat yourself up. It's a failing strategy. Your inner tyrant enjoys beating you up. It is the superego's function to tell you all the ways in which you don't measure up. You can hear the voices of the people who criticized you in the past. Your conscious mind must overrule the subconscious mind. You must reorient yourself. Are you looking at the world properly? Are you behaving in the most advantageous way? Have you set the right goals for yourself?

We will cover failure in more depth in the next chapter. For now, your task is to summon your courage to face failure while understanding that it has something of value to teach you about yourself and the world.

Struggles

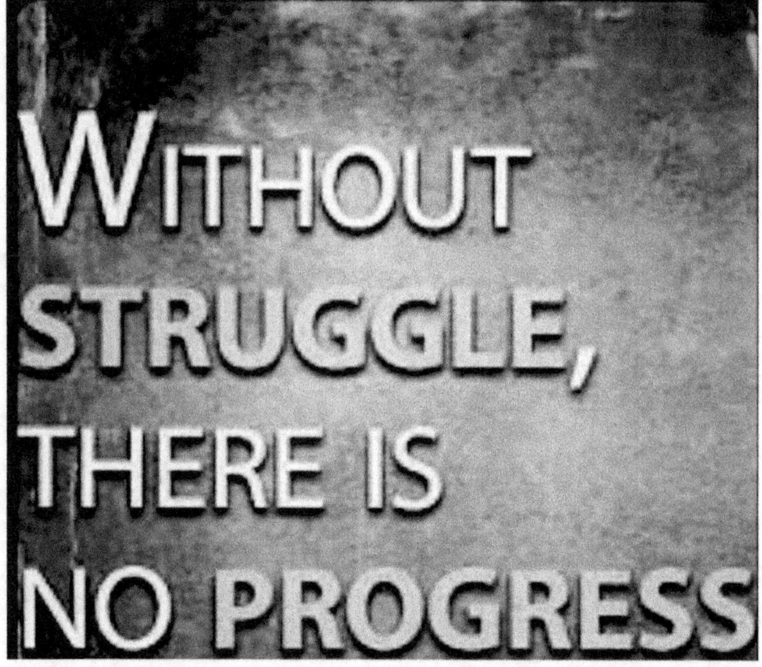

Chapter Sixteen

Frequently Occurring Pitfalls

"People are always blaming their circumstances for what they are. I don't believe in circumstances. The people who get on in this world are the people who get up and look for the circumstances they want, and if they can't find them, make them."

~ *George Bernard Shaw, Mrs. Warren's Profession*

What should you do when an obstacle arises in your life? We know that quitting is never an option. But what exactly does it mean to quit, and is there any justification for walking away from a failed enterprise?

Pay Attention

When things go wrong, and they will at one point or another, you simply need to pay attention to what part of the equation failed. Pay very close attention to it. Paying attention does not mean complaining about it. It doesn't mean beating yourself up over it. And it certainly doesn't mean finding someone to blame for it.

Paying attention means taking yourself out of the situation and looking at it as an objective third party. This is a powerful thought exercise that will help you evaluate the events of your own life with a critical eye. From this place, we can pretend that we are not personally involved and evaluate the situation as if a friend asked us for advice.

Silence!

We have talked a lot about silencing your inner critic. That inner critic does not motivate you or help you to launch. It only weighs you down by recounting your failures. In addition to shutting down the critic inside, you must shut down the critics in the world.

Perhaps you have heard of the phenomenon of crabs in a barrel. If you haven't, the theory is that crabs are so mean, hateful, and jealous that when they see another crab climbing up the side of the barrel in an attempt to escape, three other crabs will jump on its back and pull it back down. The thinking is that the other crabs are determined not to let a single crab get free if they themselves cannot get free. That is why you rarely see a lid on a bucket of crabs. It is not needed. The chances of a crab escaping are small. But there could be another possibility. Many crab species live in a community of crabs called a cast. The crabs rely on each other to survive. The bigger the community, the safer each individual crab is. When one crab tries to escape, it threatens the remaining members of the cast. Gathering food and keeping predators away is the work of the community. When the other crabs see the escapee, perhaps they are thinking of their own survival. That could be the reason the other crabs take decisive action when one tries to escape.

People are much like crabs in that way. When you are making big moves in your life, you expect the people around you to cheer you on to success. But, often, you might be shocked that the chorus of supporters is small, but the group of naysayers seems to grow. It is important not to put stock in those naysayers. It is not that they don't love you or wish you well. Instead, your escape threatens their paradigms. They have come to wear their poverty, failure, or problems like a badge of honor rather than learning the lessons you have learned to create a richer life. They don't want to invest the hard work, time, blood, sweat, and tears to change. They say it's too hard. It can't be done. And it is impossible. Your success proves them wrong and exposes their unwillingness or inability to do the necessary introspection it will take to change their lives for good. So, by trashing your success, it helps them cover their own deficiencies. Love them anyway. But don't listen to them.

Listen

Have you ever received a compliment and batted it away like a tennis ball? Just as we must silence our detractors, we must listen to our supporters and trust that they are genuine and sincere in their praise. Allow them to speak words of encouragement without talking them out of their compliment. A simple, "Thank you, that means a lot of me" is all that is required. It is not common for people to distribute words of support. So, when they do, accept them. You might find that these encouraging words bolster your resolve just when you need it most. Do not get caught in the trap of believing both the criticism and the praise. As rock legend Bruce Springsteen said:

Most artists I know had one person in their life who told them they were the second coming of the baby Jesus, and another person that told them they weren't worth anything, and they believed them both, you know?

~ Bruce Springsteen

Embrace Failure

There is only one way to overcome failure. That is to try again. Failure is not a failure unless you give up. But when you decide to try again, you condition your mind to persevere. You learn to appreciate the obstacles for how they strengthen you.

Complaining about the tough times in life keeps you locked in a negative attitude. When you learn to be thankful in all things — good and bad — you are able to maintain a positive attitude, one that has faith and trusts that He is with us in all of life's hard times. In that way, we can turn weakness into strength.

Just like you can train a weak muscle into a strong bicep, you can transform your weaknesses into strength by doing the things that are hard. A bodybuilder would lift heavier and heavier weights. With each increase in weight, the muscle has to grow. In the same way, your mind, emotions, and attitude get stronger as you do the things that are hard for you. Soon, those difficult tasks become more manageable, and you are more capable of doing more extraordinary things. Pain produces purpose, miracles come from messes, and your punishment ultimately produces peace.

Chapter Seventeen

Hidden in Plain Sight

Home is a place we all have to find. But it's not just a place where you eat or sleep. Home is knowing… Knowing your mind, knowing your heart, knowing your courage. If we know ourselves, we're always home anywhere.
~ Glenda the Good Witch, "The Wiz"

Things of beauty are often hidden deep below the surface. But sometimes, they are hidden in plain sight. What you seek is often right in front of you. But you may have been unable or unwilling to see it before some catalyst event revealed it to you. A fitting archetype of this concept is the classic story of Dorothy in the Wizard of Oz. It is a tale that has withstood the test of time, nearing one hundred years in pictures. It has been recolored and remastered repeatedly to enhance its visual and auditory appeal. However, the true magic of the story is not in the video. Instead, it lies in a powerful message for all who pay attention.

Dorothy hates almost everything about her life. She loves her family and her dog. Otherwise, the rest of her life is filled with suffering. Her parents are gone, leaving her orphaned in the care of her aunt and uncle. She lives a harsh life in the

Kansas countryside. Then, to add insult to injury, a tornado rushes through her town. She and her family run for cover, but her beloved dog slips out into the dangerous field. She rushes out in her desire to save him, unafraid to face the storm. She is indeed caught up by the tornado and transported to a magical land. Though it is a wonderful place, there are new dangers to face that she did not prepare for in Kansas. She is chased by homicidal monkeys, infected by poppies, and haunted daily by a homicidal witch who wants to see her dead.

The true power of the story occurs when she makes three friends whom she helps discover their own special gifts. It is the end of this iconic lesson in the story that you must pay strict attention to. It is Dorothy who helps her friends find their unique paths in life. She reveals to them the things they couldn't see for themselves. But for her, a question remains. It is her life's biggest question: How do I get home?

It is in this question and the answer that follows where we find a representative truth, and it is this revelation that has made this story a timeless classic. Generations from now, parents and children will continue to watch and read this story. They will treasure this tale just as we do, and the generations before us did, because it speaks to a truth that we all know on a visceral level. If we don't know it on a conscious level, we certainly resonate with the sound of truth when we hear it and see it.

The message is delivered by Glenda, the good witch, who swoops into the scene, bringing light and magic with her. Dorothy mistakenly supposes that Glenda will wave her magic wand, which is how Dorothy will get home. But instead, Glenda tells her that she never needed a witch to help her find her way home. The power to go home had been with her from the very beginning.

Home. It is one of the most comforting words in the English language. Home represents a place of security, for sure. It is where we go to escape the world and find the comforts that rejuvenate and re-energize us. But that place of security is not just intended to be a location for us to eat and rest. It is intended to be both a launching pad and a landing pad. It is the launching pad where we fire our rockets to blast off and soar. But it also serves as the landing pad where we return after our mission is completed. Once we have done our best work, we return to this place to rest, regenerate, repair, and prepare for the relaunch.

When we launch into the world, none of the comforts of home are present to bolster us. Everything in the world seems unpredictable. Things could go well, but they could also take a turn for the worst. That is what makes the quest for self so defining. It is not couched in safety. Only the brave truly venture out. Once there, they learn to be strong. The lessons of strength are not learned in the classroom; they are learned in the field. There are always scrapes, bumps, and bruises. It's part of the lesson plan. But when we return home, literally or figuratively, we have the pride of knowing we made a mark in the world.

That is the freeing truth I urge you to grasp. The power you are seeking to have, to do, and to be is already inside you, just as it was already there for the fictional Dorothy. As you move from achievement to achievement, you become stronger in the process. Bodybuilders never start lifting 1,000-pound weights. They incrementally increase as they move upwards toward their ultimate goal. The magic is in the fact that the body responds to their decision to lift more weight. The interesting and amazing thing about the body is that it doesn't crumble and give up in the presence of a heavier weight. It simply starts to build more muscle to handle the weight.

The same is true in your life overall. As an old saying goes, "Don't ask for fewer problems. Ask for more wisdom." Or, "Don't ask God to move the mountain. Ask for the strength to climb."

These great realities and discoveries about life can often sound underwhelming because they are not unique or new. They are ancient. They are truths that were discovered, I believe, by the earliest thinkers and philosophers humans have ever produced. They may be as old as humanity itself. Modern society is always in search of the newest thing. The new idea. But the best ideas are often old ideas that we have taken for granted because we have become so familiar with them. They lose their sparkle and shine because they don't have the pizazz of some new phrase.

The power to invent an amazing life is already present within you, just as it was for me. But it gets even more incredible to think about the fact that this power has been with you, inside you, all along. The meaning and purpose you crave is not off in some distant land waiting for you to search it out and possess it. It is a deep well you need to tap into.

Chapter Eighteen

Stepping into the Light

The darkness is a place we must all find and navigate. Like miners, we must delve deep into the cavern to uncover what is down there. In darkness, we discover who and what we are. We must allow the parts of ourselves to grow in darkness where they are safe to move through various changes necessary to become mature. What we find is always a great treasure that took time to create. Diamonds become diamonds, made of nothing more than carbon, through three processes: heat, pressure, and time. It takes some diamonds millions of years to form. Others take billions.

Diamonds only come to the surface when a volcano brings them up from the depths. The word diamond comes from the

Greek word adamas, which means unconquerable or invincible. Because diamonds endured such strain to come into being, they are the hardest substance we have found.

Ask any entrepreneur, actress, athlete, etc. Each of them will tell you that success happens in the darkness with heat, pressure, and time. Show me an "overnight success," and I will rewind the tape to show you years and years of struggle, work, pain, failures, and determination. The world sees them at the pinnacle of their achievement and assumes they got there quickly. That isn't true for almost anyone. I once heard a story of a girl who was singing on the New York subway and was discovered by a record producer on his way to Grand Central Station. He allegedly scooped her up, signed her to a huge contract, and she had a hit record. It's a great story. But I can't prove it's true. Even if it is true, it is only the exception that proves the rule. There is always an incubation period during which people must work, learn, stumble, fail, and grow.

Allow yourself to make all of the mistakes that are necessary to find your path. Just strive never to repeat or compound your errors. By allowing yourself to make mistakes and ensuring your mistakes are always new, you grow in your knowledge of yourself and the world.

Then, when you are ready, you can bring your treasure into the light. A concert pianist practices four hours per day alone or with a tutor over many years before she steps into the light of the stage to perform with the symphony. The gymnast practices for two hours before school and then many hours after school, on weekends, and over the summer before stepping onto the competition mat. The world's greatest basketball player, arguably, of all time, was viewed by others as an instant star with natural talent that effortlessly catapulted him to fame. What they don't know is that he practiced more than any other player on the team. He showed up so early to the practice center that they started calling it Jordandome.

> *"Compound interest is the most powerful*
> *force in the universe."*
>
> *~Albert Einstein*

Chapter Nineteen

Living in the Light of Truth

"Owning our story can be hard but not nearly as difficult as spending our lives running from it. Embracing our vulnerabilities is risky but not nearly as dangerous as giving up on love and belonging and joy—the experiences that make us the most vulnerable. Only when we are brave enough to explore the darkness will we discover the infinite power of our light."
~ Brene Brown

Pulling myself from poverty and pain to a place of wealth and comfort was not an easy trek. There are those who see me now and think this is the way it has always been. This is why I felt it was necessary to expose the truth about struggling. I am not where I am because I was spared struggle; I am where I am because of my struggle. The hard times built the strength, courage, and resilience that made me who I am today. Without the struggle, I would simply be a shell of the person I am today. That is why this book needed to be written. I needed to speak my truth and reveal the power of the struggle.

Yes, poverty, sickness, adversity, fear, and other ills of life can be painful. But we must learn to break the connection to our emotional pain and seize the power that comes from working through it.

One thing that all of the inspirational teachers and leaders have in common throughout history is the ability to express their truth. We, the masses, all look up to them as a source of inspiration, hope, and promise for a better future. But we must acknowledge that expressing your truth also means revealing your struggle. When you can be transparent with others about what you have been through, you simultaneously empower yourself and your listeners.

One tip that will help you to extract from your life all that it has to offer would be to take care of yourself. You can't do as much as you want if you are physically unhealthy. Illness in the body will affect the mind. Charity starts at home. That is no truer than with your physical body. Give the gift of self-love to yourself; you will then be inspired to give and share and contribute to those around you.

Giving to yourself means that you are living at a higher expression of truth. No lie can be greater than the lie that you can neglect your physical, mental, spiritual, and emotional health and still expect to succeed. Once you've given to yourself, you find you don't need others to agree with the decisions you make. You feel confident within yourself and don't require validation for your truth. You become the embodiment of that truth.

Your care of yourself generates greater degrees of light and love within yourself that you are able to pass to others. You can share your sadness as freely as you share your love. Living from the place of truth allows you to express your joy and spread your light. When you do, you won't feel that you are in competition or comparison with others. The only person we need to beat is the person we were yesterday.

Caring for your heart is another critical level of self-care. You learn to give love without expecting to receive anything in return. You live from a place of gratitude and joy because you feel strong in all of the important aspects of life.

Self-love is the key you have been looking for. Self-love is the key to happiness. Self-love is the key to self-empowerment. The longer we blame and judge and attack ourselves for the decisions and actions we have taken in our past, the longer we stay separated from the limitless power of self-love. The longer we hide from the darkness where we were created and formed, the longer we hide in the shadows and refuse the light.

Being truly here and now in this moment, this moment filled with limitless potential and possibility, requires us to reconnect with self-love. This is something we were all born with. However, sadly, for so many of us, the hardships we've faced in life have caused us to detach from this innate sense of self-love.

Give yourself permission to love yourself just as you are. Return to that place of self-love so that you can care properly for yourself in all the ways in which you need to, free of the past and hopeful about the future. By living and loving in the present moment, you can rebuild the broken places, heal yourself, and construct the places we truly want to live.

So much of addiction and pain are born out of a need to bury our emotional agonies and self-medicate. It stems from the need to hide the dark side. But by reconnecting to that darkness, you can learn to be grateful for it. You will arrive, someday, at the place where you can look at the trials of the past and say thank you. Thank you for the pain because through pain, I learned to heal myself. Thank you for the struggle because the struggle made me strong. Thank you for the adversity because the adversity taught me to be a problem-solver. Thank you for the rain because the rain caused me to appreciate the sunshine even more.

Congratulate yourself for being here, alive, and well in this moment. Believing in yourself and your ability is like medicine for the soul. It empowers you to face the next challenge, and the next, and the next. The darkness has taught you courage and resolve. If not for the darkness, you would be a different version of yourself. Pour out your compassion on your own beautiful soul. Congratulate yourself for surviving the darkness and for finding the beauty hidden there.

You've always done the best you could. There is no one to blame — not your parents, not your environment, not the ones who hurt you, and especially not yourself. We should not even curse the darkness because it served a powerful purpose in our lives. Self-empowerment is found in accepting responsibility for our past, present, and future. Self-empowerment is remembering that we cannot go back in time and change the past, but we can make conscious decisions in the present as we prepare for the future. We have the ability to shift our energy and state of being to the here and now. As we let go of the past and release blame, not only do we move into the present moment, but we liberate the energy that was wrapped up and bound in past hurts. Every time we switch on our survival behaviors, we draw energy that propels us toward our goals. There is no place here for guilt or resentment, blame or shame.

Many of you are familiar with the fight or flight function of the nervous system. Our hypothalamus is the part of the central nervous system that is constantly reading our environment and trying to gauge if anything threatens our safety. When the perception of a threat is picked up, it signals the pituitary gland, which signals the adrenals to mobilize energy to either fight the threat or run from it. As discussed earlier, we cannot be in survival and creation mode simultaneously. So, the longer we live in our protective, survival state, the longer we waste our energy stores turning on stress hormones.

The courage to find compassion and congratulate ourselves, just for a time, is giving us back our precious creative energy that had been diverted. As we reclaim that energy, we can use it to create a brand-new life. Breaking the addiction to our survival behaviors is the key to finding the inspiration we need to build the life we've always dreamed of.

All you have left to do now is remember those dark and lonely roads you've walked down. Yes, there were mistakes along that road. Some were made by others. Some were made by you. But there was also love and friendship on that road. There were lessons to be learned about how we might think more clearly and act more wisely. Every adversity you came up against was an opportunity. We will leave behind no undiscovered wisdom. By exercising our newfound emotional power, we can allow our consciousness to expand as we evolve to a greater understanding of ourselves, our intrinsic power, and our place in the universe.

Goodbye Yesterday

I will love the light for it shows me the way, yet I will endure the
darkness for it shows me the stars.
~ Og Mandino

It's good just to leave the past behind. You can't drag it around with you like an anvil. You can always tell the people who are tethered to the past. That anvil throws off sparks as they try to run forward. Those sparks singe everything they touch: friendships, job opportunities, romances... you name it. Everything is affected by the weight of the anvil — the past. When you try to fly, it drags you back down to the ground, reminding you of the long list of failures with your name written all over them.

Clinging to the past can cloud your vision of the present and future. You are not who you were years ago. You don't hold the same opinions. You look a bit different... feel a bit different. You have added a treasure trove of knowledge. And your life has been enriched by new experiences. The people around you have probably changed a little (or a lot). The past is not a death sentence held over your life today.

But you can only release yourself from the errors of the past when you have faced them head-on. If your past is filled with dragons in the darkness that make you shiver, they will always be there to taunt you. Just as you have a rearview mirror in your car, it is necessary to look behind you to ensure that what you have passed doesn't slam into you from behind.

What does it mean to face them? Learn the lessons they have to teach you. Each past experience says something about you, others around you, and the world-at-large. Whatever you learn serves as a building block, pushing you higher in your awareness of the world and yourself. It's hard work, I confess. Anyone who says it isn't is selling something. Don't buy it. Invest the work necessary to reconcile the past so that your life can come into balance.

When you do, you will be able to live for today instead of trying to redeem the failures of yesterday. You will be able to dream big about your future instead of carrying the baggage of the past.

I had a rough start in life, but I also had luck, for sure. The truth is that luck favors the prepared. Because I was mentally strong and ready for the adventure, I was able to seize up one opportunity after another. Everything is perfect now. My house is paid off. I have a nice pension and plenty of money in the bank. My kids are all grown up and successful. I might be tempted to consider life as a mission accomplished. But, instead, I continue to dream big. I believe that every man and woman should live fully up to the very last minute. You don't have to die in a nursing home barely cognizant of your own existence. It would be far better to leave this life doing some meaningful, exciting, or extreme.

The only way to get to this place is to shift your personal paradigm. Continue to challenge yourself to do things you never thought you would be able to do. It is good to rest, but once rested, you should get back out there and live some more so that you never become lazy. You are never, never, never too old. You may have silver hair, but you have iron will. You are strong enough to make any dream come true.

Time is an amazing element. It is the great equalizer of all humankind. You cannot buy it or sell it. The poor man cannot have it taken away. The rich man cannot barter for more. The strong man's strength gives him no advantage. Neither does the rich man's riches. Time is the only thing that is fair. As such, you might look back and worry that you have wasted time by not practicing the principles you have discovered in this book.

Fear not. Time is not the greatest asset. Timing is! For whatever reason, the universe brought this book to you. It is because your timing is just right to hear this message. Had you heard it a year ago, you might have ignored it. A year later, it might have been too late. Your time is now.

To everything there is a season,
A time for every purpose under heaven:
² A time to be born,
And a time to die;
A time to plant,

And a time to pluck what is planted;
[3] A time to kill,
And a time to heal;
A time to break down,
And a time to build up;
[4] A time to weep,
And a time to laugh;
A time to mourn,
And a time to dance;
[5] A time to cast away stones,
And a time to gather stones;
A time to embrace,
And a time to refrain from embracing;
[6] A time to gain,
And a time to lose;
A time to keep,
And a time to throw away;
[7] A time to tear,
And a time to sew;
A time to keep silence,
And a time to speak;
[8] A time to love,
And a time to hate;
A time of war,
And a time of peace.
The Bible, Ecclesiastes 3:1-8

***

Life moves in seasons. Seasons are pretty amazing if you think about it. One great feature about seasons is that each has its own unique gifts. You are especially blessed if you are fortunate enough to live in a climate with four distinct seasons. Summer brings warm temperatures with long days of sunshine. We take holidays and vacations from work and school to play and enjoy those we love. Then comes fall, when the leaves put on the most colorful show in all of nature. The reds, yellows, and oranges, mixed with the evergreens, remind us that nature is the greatest painter. Winter follows, and the ground is blanketed with snow. We become spectators of nature's wintry show as we snuggle by the fire shoulder-to-shoulder with our families. Then, spring comes to announce that everything dead must now resurrect. The trees put on their clothes, and the skies pour out refreshing rains to awaken all of nature to another year of life.

The seasons are amazing. Perhaps the greatest gift of seasons is that they come and they go. Nature is never stuck in the past. One year is unlike the next and nothing like the one before. Nature keeps moving forward. What was dead comes to life, and what has been spent lays down and dies, making way for what is to come.

The brightness of spring and summer are followed by the darkness of fall and winter. All of nature reminds us that darkness and light work in conjunction to keep our ecosystem functioning. Perhaps the greatest metaphor for darkness can be found in the night sky. What could be more wondrous than a dark night that reveals the constellations? The blackness of night is the only way to enjoy the amazing sights that are always present just above us. When the sun is shining bright, we cannot see the stars. But when the sky dims, bursts of light shoot forth, letting us know our galaxy is vast and wide.

The world's citizens have been through some tumultuous times in the past twenty years. From terror attacks to multiple dangerous diseases, including a global pandemic. That can certainly take a toll on any person's mind, body, and soul. Difficult times in our own lives or around us in the world can cause some severe side effects.

Take depression, for example. The World Health Organization estimates that 280 million are currently battling depression, and many of them rely on medication to make it through each day. Mental health crises are springing up in every country. Along with it, the use of drugs like opioids is rising. These are often used to release those feel-good hormones and create a high many people crave.

Developing coping skills is what humans do best. We learn to adapt and adjust to the most difficult events life can throw at us. But living life at the highest level is not just about adapting and adjusting. It is about thriving and flourishing. That can only be done when we are at optimal states of health, both physically and psychologically.

A major key to reaching that higher vibration relates to our energy. Your energy does not merely relate to how peppy you feel and your ability to stay awake until the end of the day. Your energy is your state of being. Energize yourself by permitting yourself to live life to its fullest, with no holds barred and no limits. Just thinking about it sends shock waves through your body now. You are free to explore all the world is offering.

Any knowledge that is not applied is nothing more than a fantasy conversation around the coffee table. Real change can only come from putting what you have learned in this book into action. Explore your own soul and unearth the treasures of desire there. Trust yourself that the things you desperately want are the things you were meant to have. This is not about material possessions, though your energy change may also bring wealth. This is about leaning into your heart's desires, maybe for the first time ever.

You are now in the driver's seat. Where will you go? What will you see? Who will be by your side? You get to decide. And when you do, you bring new energy into the world. You create something that has never existed before. You can finally be there, fully present for the people you love the most.

There is nothing to fear in the darkness. There you may find the treasure you have been seeking.

"Though my soul may set in darkness, it will rise in perfect light;
I have loved the stars too fondly to be fearful of the night."
— Sarah Williams (Twilight Hours: A Legacy Of Verse)

***

Authors portrait

Kurt Friedrich Gassner has worn many hats throughout his lifetime, including but not limited to serial entrepreneur, Creative Director, Meditation Teacher, Licensed Hypnotherapist, and more recently, self-improvement author. Leveraging his treasure trove of experiences and in-depth knowledge of psychology, he provides his readers with the tools they need to unlock their infinite potential.

As a prolific self-help writer, Kurt has authored the following books: *The Art of Forgiveness, Lie or Die, Soul-Match, Can You Inherit a Poisoned Mind?* and *The Power of Poverty*. He also authored a best-selling children's book in German-speaking countries and has over 20 books underway.

When it comes to enduring success, Kurt understands that financial prosperity isn't the only aspect one should strive for. He may be a self-made millionaire, but what really transformed his life is mastering his unconscious mind. Perseverance, personal power, self-awareness, and learning from past mistakes have all been key ingredients to bringing his dreams to fruition—and he strives to impart that wisdom onto others through his writing.

During his spare time, Kurt Friedrich Gassner is either traveling across the globe, golfing, biking in the Alps, hiking, or spending quality time with his loved ones. For the last 37 years, he has been happily married and he is the father of two successful children. Presently, he resides in both Munich, Germany, and Kirchberg, Austria.

OTHER BOOKS BY THE AUTHOR

BÜCHER VOM AUTOR IN DEUTSCHER AUSGABE

My-mindguide.com
GROW
WITH YOUR
FAILURES
GROW THROUGH YOUR FAILURES
KURT GASSNER

My-mindguide.com
WACHSE
MIT DEINEN
MISSERFOLGEN
WACHSE DURCH DEINE MISSERFOLGE
KURT GASSNER

My-mindguide.com
Lass
Los!
Verändere dein Unter- Bewusstsein, befreie dich
von materieller Abhängigkeit & wahre Lebensgeschichten
KURT GASSNER

My-mindguide.com
Let
Go
Rewire your subconscious mind with hypnosis
& cure material addiction – Real Life Stories
KURT GASSNER

OTHER BOOKS BY THE AUTHOR

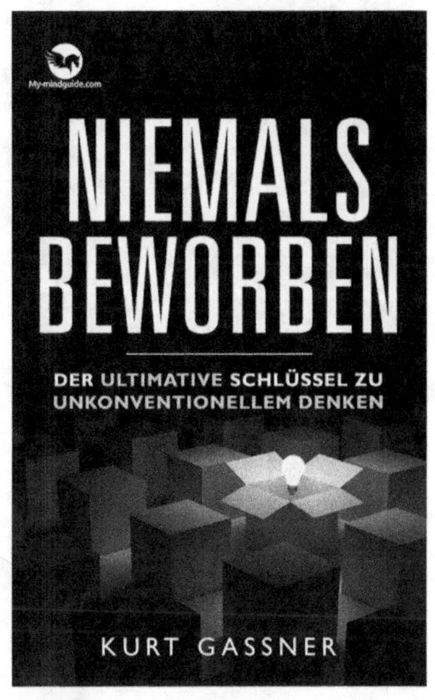

ECKO
FIRED FOR SUCCESS?
TRUE STORIES AND MANAGEMENT LESSONS
FOR OUR TOUGH CHANGING TIMES
KURT GASSNER

ECKO
WEGEN ERFOLG GEFEUERT
Eine wahre Geschichte über das Scheitern in Unternehmen und
was junge Führungskräfte aus einer Fehlerkultur lernen können.
KURT GASSNER

My-mindguide.com
Unlocking
The Healing
Power of Pets
What Pets Can Tell You About Your Soul
KURT GASSNER

My-mindguide.com
Heilkraft
Unserer
Lieblinge
Was Haustiere über Ihre Seele verraten können
KURT GASSNER

My-mindguide.com
THE
BLISS OF
STRUGGLE
WINNING STRATEGIES
FOR DEMANDING TIMES
KURT GASSNER

My-mindguide.com
STARK
DURCH
„STRUGGLES"
DAS IDEALE MINDSET,
UM KRISEN ZU MEISTERN
KURT GASSNER

My-mindguide.com
LIE LYING
& LIAR
A LIE HAS NO LEGS BUT IT HAS WINGS
KURT GASSNER

My-mindguide.com
LÜGE LÜGEN
& LÜGNER
EINE LÜGE HAT KEINE BEINE, ABER SIE HAT FLÜGEL
KURT GASSNER

BORN
in the
COLD
Liebe und Aufmerksamkeit in der Wachstumsphase eines Kindes
KURT GASSNER

BORN
in the
COLD
How to Tackle the Impact of the Absence of
Love and Attention in the Growing Stages of a Child's Life
KURT GASSNER

SOPHIAS WUNDERWELT
Erzählung & Kinatzidei in den Kitzbühler
Osterreich
10 ERZÄHLUNGEN
KURT GASSNER

SOPHIA'S WONDERWORLD
in the Austrian Alps
10 TALES
KURT GASSNER

BESTSELLING AUTHOR OF
The Art Of
FORGIVNESS
AMAZON #1 BESTSELLER
My-mindguide.com
A practical guide for self healing and overcome past traumas
The Art Of
FORGIVNESS
KURT GASSNER
The Art Of
FORGIVNESS
KURT GASSNER

9 783987 939143